"This [...]
mood[...]
rapid[...]

—TERRY RILEY, [...]

"After nearly thirty years as a musician [...]
sumed I had learned something abo[...]
chapter of *The Listening Book*, I h[...]
over. Mathieu has written a deli[...]
on consciousness, imbued thro[...]
ness, and love."

"This book is a marvelo[...]
permission to listen o[...]
W. A. Mathieu shows us[...]
rules that keep us from celeb[...]
around us and within us."

—NATALIE GOL[...]
*Down the* [...]

"*The Listening Book* is filled with charm and wis[...]
restore the spirits of the professional musician, it wil[...]
age the lay reader, and it will entertain and delight everyone."

—WILLIAM RUSSO, composer and educator

"This book turns us inside out. It makes listening itself
music."

—COLEMAN BARKS, poet

"W. A. Mathieu knows that music contains not only melody,
harmony, and rhythm, but also compassion, wisdom, and
adventure. His exciting book will help both beginners and
professionals to find new depth in the creative process."

—STUART ISACOFF, Editor, *Keyboard Classics*

"*The Listening Book* offers playful and profound suggestions
of ways of getting to the inner silence that is the source of all
music."

—MEREDITH MONK, performance artist

D0963916

# THE
# LISTENING
# BOOK

*Discovering Your Own Music*

## W. A. Mathieu

SHAMBHALA
*Boston & London*
1991

Shambhala Publications, Inc.
Horticultural Hall
300 Massachusetts Avenue
Boston, Massachusetts 02115

Shambhala Publications, inc.
Random Century House
20 Vauxhall Bridge Road
London SW1V 2SA

© 1991 by W. A. Mathieu

9  8  7  6  5  4  3  2  1

First Edition
Printed in the United States of America on acid-free paper
Distributed in the United States by Random House, Inc.,
in Canada by Random House of Canada Ltd, and
in the United Kingdom by the Random Century Group

Library of Congress Cataloging-in-Publication Data
Mathieu, W. A.
     The listening book:discovering your own music/
W. A. Mathieu.—1st ed.
          p.   cm.
     ISBN 0-87773-610-3
     1. Music appreciation.   2. Music—Instruction and study.
   I. Title.                                      90-53384
MT6.M36L6   1991                                  CIP
781.4'24—dc20                                     MN

*To Devi*

We love music because it resembles the sphere-
  sounds of union.
We've been part of an oceanic harmony before,
so these moments of treble and bass
keep our remembering fresh.

—RUMI

# Contents

Introduction   xi

LISTENING

Chop Chop Phoooah   3

The Way the Eyes Are
with the Ears   5

The Sound Horizon   6

Listening to Animals   7

Symphonies of Place   9

Protect Your Ears   13

Preparing a Sound Space   17

Focusing   19

Music at a Distance   20

Unlistening   21

Listening to People   24

The More You Listen   26

Twenty Sounds to Get Lost In   27

Special Radio Trick   29

Easy-to-Miss Music   31

Hand and Glove   33

Listening to Music   34

Dreamed Music   38

Listening to a String   39

Contents

# JOINING IN

Resonance   43

Walking   46

Singing with Machines   49

Now Time   52

Life Drummer   55

Dinner Symphony at the Sillses'   59

Gibberish   61

Say Wind   63

Chanting   66

Willing Silence   69

# PRACTICING

Finding Your Own Music   73

One Note after Another   75

Telephoning Counts   78

The Ace of Practice   80

Cosmic Practice   82

Ima Dork   83

In Meter   85

Disabusable Notions   88

The Best Excuses   90

Mistakes   92

Wandering Mind   93

No One Can Tell You   94

What Should I Practice?   95

Technique and the Eraser Trick   97

Electronic Instruments   98

Deep Pantry   100

Lentus Celer Est   101

Names   102

Chariot of Words   104

There's Not Much to Learn
   and It Takes Forever   105
Dr. Overtone's Promise   106
Originality   107

## THE SOUND CONNECTION
Finding a Teacher   113
Fear of Music   117
Hearing through Other Ears   120
Most Perfect Music   121
The Circle of Listening   123
Inner and Outer   125
Age Matters   127
Tone-Deaf Choir   128

## PRACTICES
Singing Unison with a String   137
Just Any Note?   141
As Much as Possible
   from as Little as Possible   143
Touch What You Sing   153
Steps/Leaps   157
The Tyranny of Triads   159
The Art of Returning   161
Juice between Textures   163
Play by the Clock   164
Just the News   165
The Magic Scale   166

## BIG EARS   173
Notes   178

# Introduction

Little Donald is humming and trying to enjoy it. All the other children are singing loudly. Thirty-five years later, at his wife's fortieth birthday party, Donald is still humming. He wants to sing, but he isn't singing.

Suzie, alone in her living room, is weeping at the piano. Her tears splash the white keys. She is twenty-eight, healthy, and bright. "I'll be dead before I learn this piece," she says to no one.

Jim is supposed to be loving the symphony concert, but he is rigid in his seat. He feels like a dope. He doesn't know what to listen for. There is a veil in front of the music. Of course he would never walk out, or worse, be discovered asleep by the Symphony Police.

When we are first learning to listen, the bad comes in with the good. Donald was having a great time when his kindergarten teacher told him he couldn't sing a melody; he believed her. The moment Suzie realized that she could never live up to her father's (selfish) expectations of her, her ears, born to cradle Schumann and Debussy, became paralyzed. Jim was taught early on that music is about something outside itself; now he gets tangled up in what he thinks music is supposed to be, and there is no room for listening.

There is a problem around our ears, around listening,

around music. Listening is receptive. You allow something outside your body to come inside, into your deep brain, into your private of privates. To listen is to be vulnerable. To be open and impressionable, to hear everything, is dangerous. You can be damaged all too easily.

But if you are shut tight against the world you cannot receive nourishment. The problem is how to be open enough and safe enough at the same time. The resolution is a matter of balance, of discriminating between receptivity and self-defense. This book teaches you how to listen safely and openly to the world around you. It shows you how listening can be a way of life, and how life can become musical to the awakened ear. If you want it to, this book will guide you to your own music.

*The Listening Book* is a series of connected short essays. They are arranged linearly from passive to active—from appreciation of everyday life sounds to participation in musical practices. But nature is wary of straight lines; I think we learn about listening and music the same way we learn about life and love—by skipping around. So I encourage you to sample and browse according to intuition or caprice.

I like to imagine that you will carry this book with you, in your mind as well as physically, as a companion to the stuck places in your hearing that you have also been carrying around. Later on, maybe you will contrive to lose the book for a while, then maybe find it unexpectedly in your backpack, or behind the TV. It can travel in and out of your life like an uncle, a paper uncle. Then maybe one day, when your hearing feels free and your music is flying, you will open the book and these pages will be mysteriously blank.

# LISTENING

# Chop Chop Phoooah

*Chop, chop* outside—outside someone is chopping a tree. *Chop, chop* inside—inside someone is chopping a tree. *Phooah* outside—a train whistle blows. *Phoooah* inside—the whistle blows inside a tiny world. I used to stare at the tubes around the back of our family radio, knowing that if I looked closely enough I could see miniature violinists seated in rows inside the glowing amber and flickering blues of the lighted city. Now a wee engineer in my ear is sounding the whistle again—*phoooaah*—just behind the ear drum. It's not the whistle, but the vibration of the drum itself I feel.

When you have a small new cavity in a molar, to your tongue it seems like a cave. Inside my ear canal, the tiny drum is big as a field. *Chop, chop.* I can feel the stress at the rim, where the drum is affixed, and the pattern of vibrations flowing along the membrane. In my mind I can slow these vibrations down, until I am bouncing on the surface of the drum like a kid on a trampoline. Now I'm an atom surfing through the peaks and troughs of colossal eardrum waves. No two waves are the same, no guessing at the interference patterns, just this wild riding. Suddenly a child laughs in the lane outside my window and I turn into a tingling spine, a skin washed in color. How could I have so completely become a child's laugh?

Sound is sense, and it is more intensely pleasurable the more open your ears are. Naked hearing confirms the sensual nature of the world; it is a basic act that feels good, plain and simple. Love the sensation of sound in your ears. Take

3

pleasure in hearing. Feel how the great world narrows to a flicker inside your ear, and adore how it grows into cosmos when you allow that. Be the wonder of a child hearing a bell, or music, for the first time. Feel that wonder in what you are hearing now.

Sense refines with experience, from cotton candy to hollandaise, from nursery rhymes to symphonies. Meaning occurs gradually over a lifetime, as the covenant between inner and outer matures. But the world of sense is before meaning, gives meaning to meaning. Remember to love your sense of hearing, love the echo of the world calling us awake inside our skulls. Love it now, while you read this page.

# The Way the Eyes Are
# with the Ears

The eyes are hungry. They eat brain energy. When you close your eyes your brain opens to your ears; sound rushes in to fill the sphere of the skull. Your mother's lullaby just before you drop off to sleep. Earphones on, lying on the couch, Beethoven's Seventh, your arm over your eyes. The candle sputters; lovemaking sounds in the pitch dark, then whispers and laughing.

Open your eyes: now the brain is crowded, and the bright screen of sound grows dim.

When people are listening intently with their eyes open, a strange thing happens. Their eyes roll up a little bit, and a glaze comes over them as if the surface has congealed. I love that little roll-up. Oh, those Swami Eyes! It means that the hearing, just for a moment, has become hungrier than the vision. And the way people's eyes suddenly retreat to a neutral corner when you are saying something truthful to them? That means they heard you.

And when people stare straight ahead, it means that everything is being heard and nothing is being shown. Sometimes this gaze is so powerful and beautiful that poems are written about it afterward.

Listen to the sounds you are hearing now. Then close your eyes and listen, and open them again. Try to hear the same way in both cases. Notice how the eyes are with the ears.

# The Sound Horizon

Listening into the distance is like looking into the horizon.

When we gaze at the horizon, our vision goes beyond our eyes and sees forever. When we listen into the distance, our ears reach beyond the farthest sounds, and the infinite becomes sensible. We get a fix on our position in the boundless world.

The alternative is like being stuck in traffic and never sensing beyond the stream of it. We begin to think like cars. It is like staying cooped up indoors with no windows. We need the big picture and the long radius. We need to check out the long-range coordinates.

Go out of your way, if you have to, to look steady and long at the place where earth and sky meet. Likewise, discover places where your ears can soar out to the edge of audibility. Find a lull in the evening, a valley, a distant remove, a quiet dawn, and listen into that boundary. You can disappear beyond it into where you really live.

# Listening to Animals

Dogs from Hell are barking outside. I'm in a Balinese village, it's the middle of the night, and there's nothing to do about them. They bark curses into the black sky. I roll over and concentrate on my breathing. That doesn't work. I'm wide awake with anger, resisting these demon gods, the Protectors of Wakefulness. Eyes protruding, they javelin barbed thoughts directly into my brain. Gradually, this idea of an active demon force becomes interesting. Why clench up on reality? I decide to change my tactics and actually listen.

There are three dogs roaming in the near distance; waves of others are banked back in terraced collections. As I enter the canine world I begin to hear its plain nature. The animals are at the same time frightened and protective. The near three are a clique conversing among themselves and also, as a unit, to other cliques. It is entirely a population of concerned citizens.

I become aware of their reactions and of what they are reacting to. I remember my watchdog at home. Over the years I've learned to read his barks. One combination is for cars in the driveway, one for intruding animals, another for hunger, another for cold. I can sometimes identify the person arriving or the kind of animal by the quality of the bark. Tonight I am far from home, in strange fields, but in these new voices I can read unseen nocturnal messages: odors on the wind (human and otherwise), disturbances in the insect pattern, the single footfall that doesn't fit the expectation, the need for reassurance. Turf is taken through a puff of the lungs and a scrape of the larynx. Short barks are words clustered in staccato sentences. Howls are poems careening over the air waves. Absorbed and hypnotized, I eventually fall asleep listening to late-night dog radio.

Once I was feeling sorry for a lion in the zoo. I was also getting a big charge from examining him up close. As he paced ten feet away, I sketched the outline of his terrifying shape intimately in my eye, storing up his ferocity for later.

The lion stopped and stared me down; I gazed bravely in return. He growled suddenly, not stupefyingly, just a mezzo forte "this is who I am" growl. Because I was already entranced, my ears were open, and I heard the sound as if he had drawn, in splended detail, the dimensions of his insides. I saw the rib cage and the hollow volumes of all the cavities, the lungs and the gut and the bowels, red in the dark, all posed for the portrait. "This is a sound picture of my body," said the lion, "a transmission of my being into yours. Believe it!" He was turned inside out as simply and completely as a pair of trousers.

I have a cat who talks. She is eighteen years old, arthritic and half blind, but her large vocabulary of pleas and purrs come in rapid cadence, especially when you alternate yours with hers. In my pre-lion days I would think up amusing English analogues for her words. Now I hear her body turned inside out. No need for English—the communication is direct and complete.

You can become your cat when you listen deeply to her voice. With a little courage you can be the lion. You can even be the Dogs from Hell, busy delineating the boundary between their collective insides and the reality of midnight. When you understand the language, you are rooster, pig, and goat. Part of you leaps to life for a moment's appreciation of purr, yowl, crow, squeal, or bleat. That sound is the bridge that leads you out of your skin and out of your cage.

# Symphonies of Place

At home in Sebastopol, California. I am writing at the kitchen table, my right ear next to the open window; it hears outside sound, mostly. My left ear hears sounds coming from the kitchen, and the rest of the house beyond. Immediately I notice my noisy refrigerator motor is OFF, at least for the time being. It is a bright midday in June. The temperature dial says 66.

Three or four noisy crows are circling.

A car whizzes up the hill.

The swish of my felt-tip pen on legal paper.

The skin sound of my right hand as it slides across the paper.

My wife, Devi, is eating breakfast in her office down the hall. The spoon against the cereal bowl: metal and crockery.

The intermittent rattle and thump of her computer keyboard: she thinks, she types.

There are several kinds of birds, I don't know their names: *peep peep, warble, chip chip.* Now I recognize the call of the Swainson's thrush rising from the creek on the other side of the house.

Wind in the nearby apple trees.

Fast little forays of flies—there are two in the room. Each buzz lasts for about one second, begins high and ends lower. Do they rev down for landing?

Now there is a special bonus: from the fire station a mile east the noon siren goes up, stays level for three seconds, and gently decays into all of the above.

A car goes by too fast for the two-lane blacktop. High whoosh of air. Tire noise. As it labors uphill around the first bend its metal throat explodes open. Around the second bend two tires shriek at once, a twinge of white dissonance.

An airplane is droning on a straight path, not near.

There is a single world-class ding from the best wind chime I ever heard—a wedding gift from Anna and Richard.

Our aging cat utters a soft meow of complaint that somehow reminds me of my Grandma Clara, long dead.

In the lulls I hear traffic from the through road, two miles north.

Our dog is lying half-asleep under the quince bush. When he stirs I hear his fur against the grass.

My breathing.

I am now aware of two cicada type of insects, both scraping their knees. In front of me, nearby, is the slower one; the one behind me is faster, but farther away. I don't know how long they have been singing.

I absent-mindedly rub the fingers of my left hand together: the high-pitched swish of skin on skin. My knuckles creak: I am so protective of my piano hands that the sound makes me uptight. I put my left hand against my face and rub the stubble of beard; now that *is* a weird sound.

Wind in distant trees.

Now Devi's computer printer suddenly starts to whine.

The refrigerator motor lumbers back on, and I'm going to walk the dog.

Get a pencil and paper. Become aware of all the sounds you are hearing now, this moment, as you read. Make a list of them. Close your eyes from time to time. Swivel your head slightly to change the mix. Make a sweep from nearby sounds to distant sounds. Fall into the distance. Become transparent. Now fall into the nearness. Make a sweep from the highest sounds to the lowest ones. Disappear into the stratosphere, reappear underground. If your space is quiet enough you will hear your own internal sounds: breathing, maybe your blood in your ears. Or the subtle sounds of cloth against cloth, skin against skin. Count everything; write everything down. Use words economically. Later, if you like, you can set the scene and go into detail.

Now make your sweeps into scans so rapid that you have the illusion of hearing everything at once. Now close your eyes and hear everything at once. Now cup your hands behind your ears. Technicolor!

This is the sound of your now, your Symphony of Place.

Here is another one of mine.

SYMPHONY NUMBER 2

Downtown Santa Rosa, California. It is a summer evening—after dinner but still daylight. I am on the perimeter of a pedestrian area surrounded by shops, a restaurant, and a movie theater, sitting on a stone ledge near the theater entrance. I hear the footsteps of a couple passing by. The guy's keys hit against his belt.

Thirty yards away, city traffic: light trucks and cars.

The big glass doors of the theater open with a squeak and close with a whoosh and a click.

The high whine of an engine.

A truck tailgate slams open.

A car starts.

Three small kids pass, with Mom: their footsteps and a plaintive, muffled request.

Low conversation nearby.
Running footsteps, tennis shoes.
Wind in trees.
The pages of my writing pad rattle in the wind.
In anger a woman shouts, "What!"
A small child calls, "Wait!"
A group of men is talking across the courtyard.
Nearby, one man mutters something.
Some kids far away.
Someone is calling "Kevin" many times.

Devi knows I'm writing down sounds in my book. Now she crosses my line of vision, pawing at the cement like a pony.

Our laughing.
Sandals shuffle.

The squeak in the door has developed into a long followed by a short.

S sounds from a conversation.
More laughing from somewhere else.

A uniformed theater sweeper sweeps; the plastic broom bristles go *sweep sweep*; his plastic trash catcher scrapes against the cement.

Plate glass creaks in the wind.
A proud voice booms, "You did it!"
More keys jingling in step, fading.

# Protect Your Ears

Here are some stories about ears.

When I was nine my mother took me across town to hear a string quartet—my first chamber music. The performance was at night. I was tired after a school day, but I listened attentively like she told me to all through the Mozart, which I loved, and the Schubert, which made me sleepy. Then came the pièce de résistance, the real reason Mom had brought me out at night, the confirmation of our Hungarian heritage: Béla Bartók's Fourth String Quartet. Her cheeks glowed as she told me to sit up and listen.

This is the quartet with a lot of sliding, sharp-edged glissandi. I was a good little boy and opened my ears all the way. What I heard was at first shocking, as though something were terribly wrong, like an air raid. But everyone sat still as church. When the glissandi began, there were curved white pains in my ears. I cried out in dismay. I had been prepared for something nice, and then it wasn't nice, like bitter candy. Mom did her best to make me brave, but soon she was leading me out, past everyone's tucked-in legs. In the car I put my head on her lap, and her hand over my ear, and my hand over her hand, all the way home.

When I was seventeen, in my first year at the University of Chicago, I fell in love with a girl who taught me to hear sounds that were loud and difficult. Beyond their loudness and difficulty was a kind of beauty she longed for. Would I

13

care to accompany her to the library to listen to Schoenberg string quartets?

In the diffused winter light of the listening room we sat for two hours holding hands, dissonance streaming through our earphones. Though my teenage ears were affected by the Schoenberg the same way my boyhood ears had been affected by Bartók, my response was different. I didn't tighten up against the harshness. I learned to relax and allow the sharp edges to pass through me like wind through fiber. This opened a new world of music and of sound. I got into the habit of standing beneath the elevated tracks of the Illinois Central Railroad at Fifty-fifth Street and letting the long cacophony of the trains thrill my bones.

A dozen years later, in 1967, I moved to San Francisco and went to hear rock bands at the Fillmore. I hooked into the singing of Janis Joplin, and one Sunday matinee decided to see what would happen if I stood two feet in front of a speaker twice my height and cranked to the max. Two things happened: I experienced a blend of ecstasy and pain so intense that I will remember it forever. And I went a little deaf.

A tough lesson. But I learned that the ear is a haven. I learned how the mother has to protect the womb, how delicate is the egg of the ear.

How can one be open and closed at the same time? How to let inside what is good and useful and keep outside what hurts you? How to exclude the bad stuff without shutting yourself off from life? The answer is: discrimination, and good judgment. Discrimination means knowing what is good for you and what is bad. Good judgment means knowing when to duck.

14

OLD JOKE

> STUDENT: O Guru, what is the secret of life?
>
> GURU: Good judgment.
>
> STUDENT: How do you get good judgment?
>
> GURU: Experience.
>
> STUDENT: How do you get experience?
>
> GURU: Bad judgment!

Pay attention to what you are hearing, what you are subjecting your ears to. You have to know when to say "come in" and when to say "stay out"; that is basic to life. What is not obvious is how to do it consciously, deliberately, with your sense of hearing.

When you carry an infant around with you, cradling it against the world, you come to understand the equation between its vulnerability and your caring. When you cradle your ears they become increasingly precious to you, and you seek out new ways to give them love.

Protecting yourself against unwanted sound means, for one thing, carrying earplugs. They cost a couple of bucks at your drugstore. I do this, and I use them when the sound level becomes threatening. It also means not being too shy or embarrassed to hold your hands over your ears, or put your fingers in your ears, when sound is suddenly too loud.

Even when sound isn't life-threatening it can still be too loud. Don't be afraid to ask the waitress to turn down the sound system. Stand up for your rights. When my dentist sees me coming he turns off the Muzak. ("It's such a relief when you're here," whispers the hygienist.) It's even all right to ask your friends nicely to turn off the TV they haven't been watching. And if there is nothing to be done at the moment, it's OK to walk out, to give ground, to abandon the mall, to leave your neighborhood for the woods. You're not crazy. Sometimes leaving is a victory. You have to know when.

What about angry noise? Some people use their stereo as a weapon. Should you transmute their rage? Transcend it? Confront it? Put in the plugs? Bake them some cookies? Take a walk? Call the cops? Move? My meaning is that you should do something, and care what you do. For the sake of your hearing, discriminate. And take action, even if that means only taking a deep breath. Don't give up and let your ears gradually grow closed. You can always find a way of upgrading the sound in your space, or your perception of it, if you care enough.

And when you do care, the reward is so precious. Murmurs. Lullabies. Rain. Waves of cicadas under the moon. Your own tenderness for yourself. Be a fierce protector; it is the road to being an open listener.

# Preparing a Sound Space

You don't have to have an altar to pray or a special place to practice listening. There are monks who meditate in Grand Central Station. Adepts are always in their sound space, or so I'm told. But temples *can* make you feel holy, and it is useful to have a sound temple, a trusted place where you can let sound all the way in and listen all the way out.

Any place that pleases you is good. Maybe you won't have to look far. Your sound space could be your bed, or a corner of your living room. Maybe you'll have to adjust something for a few minutes, pull the plug of the refrigerator (don't tell a soul, and be sure to replug). Or wait until the kids have piped down a bit. Or wait until the neighbor's stereo is off. Maybe you'll have to get the jump on the natives by waking up earlier. Maybe you'll even have to travel some. But sitting quietly in a place where ambient sounds don't trigger negative responses is worth the effort of getting there.

If you look for such a spot you will no doubt find it. People have the habit of going to the country, of seeking out wilderness. But you can find a little wilderness of your own wherever you are.

WHAT IS OK IN YOUR SOUND SPACE

- ° Sounds of nature
- ° Live sounds, including speech, especially at some distance

- Lots of different kinds of sounds, including traffic, or even those listed below, if these are sufficiently diffuse or distant not to offend you or hook you into their drama

## WHAT IS NOT OK IN YOUR SOUND SPACE

- Recorded music or anyone practicing music
- Any radio or TV
- Unrelenting mechanical noise
- Anything unpleasantly loud or close, or that makes you uncomfortable

The idea is to create a space that not only protects you from unwanted sound but also releases you from any impulse to close your ears. The exercise is to open up, and wherever you can do that best is your sound space.

# Focusing

It's midnight. You are alone. New cabin. Strange woods. Out of the night, a cry. What was it? Your ears strain. Every sound, even the silence, is animated by curiosity, perhaps by fear. It is as though your ears are listening through a microscope, and you hear what you've always heard, except to the tenth power.

Now you are cruising down the freeway and there is a new buzz in the engine. Or is it the glove compartment? Or that truck passing? For a few moments your ears snorkel into the ocean of mechanical noise to find the one fishy clink that hasn't been there before.

Now the phone rings. The person asks for you and says, "I bet you can't guess who this is—you haven't heard my voice in twenty years," and a whole world of memory rushes in through one ear.

When you need to, you can focus utterly on sound. Musicians learn to do it as part of their training. It becomes habit. But anyone who wants to can practice it.

It's easy.

Just pretend that your life depends on the next sound you hear.

# Music at a Distance

Hearing sounds over long distances takes us out of ourselves and out of the daily frame.

A sound mirrors the shape of its container. The sound of a church bell in a valley reflects the shape of the whole valley. A shout from the ridgetop visits all the slopes. As sound is diffused and softened through space, so, when we listen to it, is our sense of self. We are spread out over the land, rarefied, free at last. Distance lends yearning to sound. From far off, even the sound of city traffic has a kind of longing in it.

I have a daydream of making music for very loud acoustic instruments heard over long distances. We would build machines: enormous, remote-operated bellows-driven whistles and reeds and horns. There would be gigantic bells of every tone, far-reaching drums, and pounded metal and stone. All of these would be at one end of a valley rimmed with ridges on which we would stand and hear the whole symphony from a half mile away. Real compositions, too, the morning long; or dusk music. Acoustic Music Over Long Distances: AM-OLD. I want to hear it at least once—for once, to get enough of that airy, spacious power.

# Unlistening

I am sitting above the swimming pool on a restaurant veranda in Penestanan, Bali. I am writing this book, this very chapter in fact, about listening from the seat of detachment; cool listening, Zen listening. Someone inside a nearby bungalow is practicing Balinese wooden flute, only three notes: *do*, *re*, *mi*. There is no one in the pool, no one in the restaurant except me, no one visible in the surrounding bungalows. I am alone with my thoughts, my notebook, and this novice flutist. He is practicing the three notes in every possible combination, ceaselessly, until I lose my grip on my writing. My teaching hackles are up. "You're missing the point," I lecture him to myself. "The essence of music is the sound of it, and you're stuck on a problem of combinations. You're not even hearing what you're playing. Enter into the sound. Then the music will come and I can get on with my work."

At this moment, a rooster crows in the middle distance and the *mi* of the flute makes an astonishing, protracted unison with the *doo* of the *cock-a-doodle-doo*. Then the rooster adds a ringing upper grace note to his *doo*, flinging my ears outward to a larger sphere. The rooster, the flute, the lapping of the pool, the breeze, all are now waves in a pattern of beautiful waves. My pencil's writing is part of the same symphony as the student's practicing. One intention. One wave-ocean. To be part of that wave-ocean, while at the same time perceiving it, is a sublime moment of clear hearing. That moment has made my world whole.

I want to know how to live in that world.

The rooster helped me this time. He was the catapult that took me beyond my little teaching into the big teaching of sound. But it can be done without a rooster.

There is a hearing meditation that has two parts: first you unlisten; then you listen.

Unlistening means clearing sounds from their associations, which are often unconscious. Make them conscious. If bird song means replenishment, know that. If the sound of traffic makes you shrivel inside, know that. Somewhere along the line I got the idea that the garbage man was going to come inside my house and beat me up, so fear is my association with the sound of the early-morning garbage truck. Maybe it is not possible to strip all the layers of meaning away from sounds, but at least you can evaporate the surface thoughts. The more completely you do this, the more deeply sound will enter you and reveal its true nature. The act of identifying your psychological response is a ticket to an even deeper response.

Some sounds will never become unglued, nor should they. Too-loud or life-threatening sounds better stay that way. And words spoken directly to you.

Once you have identified an association, shoo it away. Choose to listen past it into the world of sensual vibration. It's amazing how the pitch and roll of thinking dulls the ear. When thinking calms down, even a little bit, sound wakes up. This sudden aliveness may have happened to you spontaneously in a moment of danger (no time to think) or in a trough of absent-mindedness. But you can intentionally stimulate its happening by being quiet (standing in line, sitting at your desk, lying awake) and drifting down through the cloud cover of mental associations onto the surface of the vibrational world.

It might take only a moment to drop in. Or it might take many moments of slippery wrestling. But the nature of sound works in your favor and rescues you time and time again from the tether of the mind.

There is a wonderful movie called *Call to Glory* about the work of Sufi teacher Samuel Lewis, who taught joy by experiencing it with his students. One day during the making of the movie it seemed like a good idea to go up to the top of the hill near Sam's San Francisco house and film him singing a call to prayer. So up everyone climbs to the bald little summit. Just as the shot is being made, a bunch of kids zoom by on their dirt bikes, two-stroke engines roaring like dragons. But Sam keeps right on calling the prayer at the top of his lungs and the cameraman keeps on filming. Did the teacher hear the motorcycles? Of course. He heard them as part of the life he was celebrating, the very part he was celebrating at that moment. When you watch the movie, which begins with this scene, it is comical to see a little old man with his hands cupped in back of his ears singing away while biker kids circle around them. It is also illuminating because, in the receptive state of the teacher and the photographer, "roll 'em" transcended "cut," and the scene became complete.

# Listening to People

You can tell a lot about a person by a single spoken word—like *hello*—even if that person has a mask, or layers of them, as most of us do. After all, what could be more revealing than the mask one wears? Speech is so direct, such a complete turning outside of what is inside, that to try to mask it is to reveal more of the whole.

Some people are disturbed to hear their own voice played back on a tape recording. It's like catching a glimpse of yourself in the mirror at a party: Who is that stranger?

It is difficult to know objectively the sound of your own voice. But it becomes easier as you learn to hear the voices of others more fully. Real strangers can help you. Listen openly to people speaking in a foreign language. Beyond the words is the true meaning. Understand the speakers by the sounds they make. Sweet folks, critical ones, cunning or defensive ones. The pure sound of a sympathetic heart. Or listen to English being spoken while pretending you don't know the language. Listen to friends and pretend they are strangers in a strange land.

Listen to people with detachment, without wanting a certain thing to be so, without judgment, just for the practice of it. What you will hear is the cadence of desire on their voices—the rising and falling prototype of musical cadence. It is there, raw, every time someone speaks. "Tonal" languages, like Chinese, seem almost sung. Singing is in fact the extension of the tonal impulse that arises in speech. All languages are tonal in the sense that rising and falling pitch mirrors the tide of feeling in the heart.

Even the monotone of the lecturer on statistics shows by its variegations of gray the desire for the rainbow trapped inside, just like a faded monochrome can leave a more vivid impression than a color movie. Maybe beneath the lecturer's mask lies a secret passion for numbers.

But to hear the passion, you have to take yourself out of the equation. Listen empty. When your critical mind disappears, other people's speech takes on the pristine clarity of pre-language.

Noncritical listening is the way to learn the sound of your own speaking voice. You have to listen to yourself with dispassion, at a cool remove. Your voice will then be your best helper, your intimate friend. The stranger in the mirror will become your confidant, the one who unveils you and protects you at the same time.

This takes a little practice. And a little courage, like diving; but unlike diving you can do it anyplace or anytime. Try it with the next word you speak.

# The More You Listen

We can no more hear all the vibrations in a sonata than we can see all the radiation from the stars. There is an effulgence, a surfeit in the world. We will never hear it all, even if we invent a hundred new ways to listen and bring all the dark into the light. There will always be more. Waves make waves and draw our senses in beyond limit.

It was a great day when I discovered that there is more in the air than I had ever heard before, or ever could hear. I remember the amazement in realizing "the more you listen the more you hear," the delight in registering sounds that had always been present but I had never heard, the ecstasy of knowing this is a lifelong experience, infinitely expandable, basically musical. I spoke wildly to my friends. I began inventing exercises and games to trick people into hearing more so I could experience the freshness of their wonder. I never stopped doing it. I'm doing it now.

# Twenty Sounds to Get Lost In

Obviously, wind chimes; they can lead you to unexpected pleasure.

Two music boxes, or three, at once.

Rain.

River; waterfall.

Crickets; FROGS.

Wind around corners.

Your own breathing.

People hammering at a construction site: the cross rhythms.

Radio tuned between two music stations so you can hear both equally.

"Station X": the pure static between stations on radio or TV.

Water in a pipe: toilet filling; the sound of a shower.

Playgrounds: children at a distance.

Wind in leaves.

The street: listening from one spot.

Foreign-language conversations.

Echo.

Log fire.

Flagpole: the wind in the flag, the rope on the pole.

Your hair being rubbed against your scalp.

Shuffling cards.

That's twenty, but I don't want to stop!

Crackling cellophane.

Aluminum soft drink cans when you squeeze them just a little bit.

Don't forget birds.

A fan of Grand National Stock Car Racing just before the green flag at the start of a race: "I can't wait to hear when they open up. It's like good sex."

# Special Radio Trick

Advertisers who buy time on the air have a small but real advantage over us: we don't like to interrupt our rhythm by turning down the radio. They have a right to advertise, of course, just as I have the right to listen or not. And some commercials are in fact amusing, striking the fine balance between salesmanship and good taste. But all of them want you to do something. Even if your ears have stopped hearing, that manipulative energy becomes part of your living. The energy of nonlistening—of ignoring something—becomes part of you.

Television consumers have partially solved this problem with remote control devices. Most of us radio listeners, however, still have to reach for the knob; few of us bother. I listen a lot—sports, news, talk shows—and have built a sixty-second timer into my brain. I can turn down the volume and turn it up again sixty seconds later, by reflex. It has become a habit. By this means I've spared myself, over a finicky lifetime, one solid lunar month's worth of radio commercials. *Reach for the knob*, I say.

Advertising is a subtle and pernicious abuse. The danger is not so much in being hustled as in the unconscious shield we build up against being hustled. We sink into an ear coma; there is already enough phasing-out in civilized life. If I have the option to upgrade my sound space, I want to recognize that option and use it. Given the choice, I'd rather hear than not hear.

I'm proud of my sixty-second timer, the absence in my life of people selling me things continuously, though I realize that my pride is just the other side of their ambition.

Meanwhile, I'm reaching for the knob. I don't need a market in my ear. Wind is better.

# Easy-to-Miss Music

A few seconds after you turn on a fluorescent light there are two or three quiet little pings, its signature tune. Sometimes very musical.

Ping-Pong balls have a musical pitch every time they are struck; a game becomes musical when you listen to that. If you let a Ping-Pong ball bounce itself out on cement it makes another kind of music. If you trap the ball with your paddle into a smaller and smaller bounce, the bounce gets faster and higher pitched until it disappears with a kind of choking sound. One afternoon when I was seven I found this so funny I got sick from laughing.

Pages being leafed through.

Next time you unfurl some new tinfoil, don't cut it off the roll immediately. Hold it close to your ear and move it slowly.

Form your tongue as if to say the letter s and then minimally whisper it. Move the tip of your tongue around until you have found your private flute music.

Bullet casings make neat whistles when you blow across the tops of them like panpipes. So do pen caps, bottles, and anything else tubular.

Fingers and palms and hands rubbing together, held up to the ear.

Coat hangers jangling together.

Wrap the middle of a two-foot length of thread around the hook of a coat hanger so that about twelve inches of thread extends equally from each side. Wrap each end of the thread around a little finger and put your little fingers in your ears, the coat hanger suspended below your nose. Cause the coat hanger to strike a metal object. You will hear a gong. You can do the same thing with oven grates. (Devi says, "Oven grates are better than coat hangers by a billion miles!")

Before you throw away your next burnt-out light bulb, hold it by the metal base close to your ear and shake it.

The way the pitch changes when you fill a metal pan (or anything) with water.

Add to this list.

# Hand and Glove

At the moment of creation, sound was the same gleam in the eye that you were when your parents first thought of you. Long after creation, there appeared solid bodies that knew how to vibrate and, even later, air to carry their messages. And only much later, but still from the same lineage, did the ear appear as a receiver of messages. A receiver is the complement of what is received, like the vortices in a seashell are the complement of the vortices in water. Sound and the ear have complementary natures; they reflect each other. Sound is hand, ear is glove.

So in the act of hearing, you experience a part of the creation that made you, something that has been alive from the very beginning, something you almost remember. Sometimes when you listen to music you could swear you actually do remember. The music lets you witness the original spark. Each tone becomes a metaphor for the moment of your origin. "You never lose it," the music says, "no matter how long it's been gone. It's here now, here now."

# Listening to Music

Music reflects the purpose it was made for. The textures and structures of dance music are different from those of mystery movie scores. Dance music wants to have a wedding with your body. Mystery music wants to scare you out of your mind. There is music to watch a play by, music to be romanced by, dinner music, theme music, advertising music, patriotic music, music to get lost in space by, music to fill-in-the-blank by. Pretty far down the list for most people is music to listen to.

Nothing is wrong with stories or movies or dancing or daydreaming or thinking. They all mix in their enjoyable ways with music. But none of them is the same as listening to music. If you have yet to listen to music without one of the above, a fine new experience is ahead of you.

There is a funny story going around about New Age music. A diner in a restaurant says to the waiter, "The needle is stuck on that record you're playing." The waiter replies, "No, it isn't stuck, it's New Age. It only *sounds* repetitive to the unsophisticated ear that doesn't know how not to listen to it . . ."

The truth is, most of us have to learn specifically the single, pure act of listening to music. Sometimes music does come to you by itself, unexpectedly surrounding you. Startled, you wake up in a beautiful new house of sound. But for the most part, learning to listen takes time and patience, like training a small muscle. This is what musicians do to learn their trade—they practice listening, with ever-deepening concentration and perception.

Music that is meant to be listened to for itself, and not as an accompaniment to anything else, is called absolute music. Finding some that you like might not be so easy. You need music that beckons to you, holds you in its sphere, and shows you something hidden in yourself. The most accessible classical music is generations behind us. North Indian music is half a planet away. Contemporary art music comes in untested bins. Yet there is enough incredibly fine absolute music in the world to allow any seeker to eventually build up a list of preferences.

My current "Best Listening List" contains much Bach; some Mozart and Beethoven string quartets; some Terry Riley; some Middle Eastern, North Indian, and Bulgarian music; some Stan Kenton and Miles Davis . . . but this is not your list, it's my list. All my life I've been looking for music that I trust as much as a country boy trusts his swimming hole, so that every dive can be carefree and perfect. My list works for me. No one can tell you what should be on yours. That is what makes your list valuable.

What makes it so difficult to simply listen to music? The problem is thinking. Thoughts are famished and your brain is food. When thoughts are feasting, it is difficult to hear over the din and commotion of the banquet.

There are many kinds of thinking, and listening is not any of them. There is the kind of thinking where we work out our plans for the day, or for our lives. Remembering is a kind of thinking. So is fantasizing. There is also the kind of thinking that places experience in context and explains its meaning. There is analytical thought, which takes apart what it is experiencing, and holistic thought, which connects it to cosmos. Any of these modes of thought can be a response to music or can be intensified in the atmosphere of music. None are necessarily to be avoided. But each in its way is an arm that holds you back from the embrace.

People are taught that they can understand music only if they know something about it. Understanding music means knowing how many kids Bach had, or knowing about Mozart's relationship with his father, or which sound is the oboe d'amore, or where the recapitulation occurs. There is something in this. But in my view, music is intellectually illuminated from within. It is itself a radiating mind that illuminates yours by resonance. It needs only your consciousness of its streaming for it to become absolutely what it is. It needs only to be heard.

Learning *about* music is a matter of doing your homework. Surely it is useful to study the history of a new town the better to enjoy your visit there; and knowing the layout of the streets does help you get around. But knowing these things is not the same as experiencing the town. Some tourists memorize the history and the points of interest and never leave the tour bus. A conscious traveler can get the feel of a new place just by being there, by sitting in the café with an open mind while the town comes alive.

Here is how to listen to music with your whole self. Find the right piece of absolute music. Find an undisturbed setting, be it a concert hall or your own room. As you listen, be as comfortable as possible. Close your eyes. Relax your forehead. Perhaps you will see shapes—benign, abstract, light-filled forms—which are a neurological aspect of the sound. There will be pictures *of*, and thoughts *about*, and twitches and itches and physical responses. Don't fight these; just keep coming back to the sound. Grab onto any aural feature—the clarinet, the cello, the cymbal—to pull yourself back. Focus on what you are hearing and enter in, no matter what. Inhale music and exhale music. Nothing is needed except awareness and your desire to let the music be your whole reality. With the regularity of a heart beat, keep returning to the sound and the sound alone. All parts of it. Scan it high and low. Be starved for it. Let it be starved for you.

Here is a good practice using recorded music. Get a clean copy of a short piece (three to six minutes) of instrumental music that you can listen to wholeheartedly—classical, jazz, country, rock, anything you love—and play it twice in a row every day for about five days. Don't do anything else when you listen to it: no read, no look, no sing, no think, no dance, no dream, no scheme, no mad, no paranoid, no fantasy, no memory, no nuthin'. Get into a daily rhythm of pure, clear-channel listening.

This sounds like a sales pitch, and it is. As a culture we have forgotten how to listen to music. Music has become devalued currency, ubiquitous and banal. I'm glad that music is everywhere. I'm not glad that the purpose of its being everywhere is to sell you something, like records, for instance, or more food at the store. In less civilized cultures music is everywhere because all the people make it. Singing, dancing, clapping, drumming, and playing instruments are ways of being together, or of being alone. But most of what we hear in our culture is recorded. Music has become a specialty given over to professionals. Even though it seems like music is closer to us because it is everywhere, it is actually farther away.

So your personal discipline of listening to music is not only a step up for your own consciousness. It is another way of refusing to be an undiscriminating consumer. If you know what it is to really hear music, it will be that much tougher on the next guy who tries to sell you a microwave with a rude jingle. Being a conscious consumer of music elevates the quality of music everywhere.

# Dreamed Music

"I dreamed I wrote a symphony, but when I woke up I couldn't remember it. In my dream I was in the audience. Then I was conducting the orchestra. Then I was floating downstream on a river barge while along the banks curving lines of musicians played the score in perfect stereo. I could hear the resin on the bows of the violins. Thrilling, high trumpets. Real cannon for drums. If only I could remember the music. If only I could write it down."

No one can tell you what you really hear when you dream music. The impression can seem more vivid than music, as if coming from somewhere inside it. But the stuff of dreams is more rarefied than the stuff of music. The vibrations are finer, more like feeling than sound, more like the inhalation of a poet before she speaks a line than the spoken line itself. Just as dream light is soaked up in the light of day, dream sound is lost in the noise of wakefulness.

Don't long for lost music. You can't capture your dream symphony and bring it back alive to the conscious, rational world. But you can often clearly remember how the music made you feel. Go for the real meaning of the dream. Go for the feeling.

# Listening to a String

Pluck a string on the guitar, or strike a key in the midrange of the piano. Listen to the tone with open ears until it is completely gone. Don't give up listening too soon; wait until nothing sensible remains of the original stroke. Notice how thoughts crowd in, and notice the various stages of their evaporation. Musical tone can boil thoughts away. This is the open secret of making music. Set the string to vibrating again, lock your hearing onto its energy and be absorbed into its disappearance. You will always get something back from this piece of work. Like a good vacation, being there is the reward for getting there.

A stretched string shows how music transforms energy. Compare ocean water whipping about on a windy day with water streaming through a high-pressure hose. Within the hose the water's energy is aligned. The force of a finger's pluck or hammer's stroke is confined and channeled by a string in the same way. The trapped force becomes a musical vibration that dissipates gradually. A sudden blow becomes calm radiance. We never tire of this transformation, and cause it to happen again and again, millions of times. String sound is downright pleasurable, more and more so as we learn to concentrate on it. We love its subtle magic. Order appears out of thin air. When you identify with the sound you become likewise ordered by a kind of resonance. You are tuned by the string. Your hidden string speaks. This is the original language you've forgotten. As listening itself becomes hollow like a flute, the source language returns. Meaning pours from it. You remember your ancestors, not just the humans or the apes or the fishes, or even the gases and fires of creation, but the vocabulary out of which creation learned to be.

As a string tone gets softer, its energy radiates over a wider area. When it is no longer audible it doesn't cease existing, but keeps changing form, into heat and other kinds of radiation. If you stay with it into the silence, it might take you along with it as a passenger. Don't worry about coming back; everyone eventually does.

The history of music is the history of our response to tone, our waking up to it, our remembering and forgetting it, our becoming it in human form. Each time you hear a tone more clearly than the last time, you participate in the Great Remembering. It is collective, but it is simultaneously private and intimate. Your experience of tone is unique and secret.

So try it again: get quiet; then the pluck or the stroke; then the long decay of sound into space. Two more times. Be patient. This is the best preparation on earth for making music.

# JOINING IN

# Resonance

Like things vibrate alike.

Realizing that.

Walking with my buddy, swaying in step. Clapping with the crowd in time to the band. Dancing at the disco. Making love like a single beast. Timing my breath to the breakers on the beach. Breathing in unison with a circle of friends. Home run at the ball park—fifty thousand screams of joyous aggression. Waking up glad to be alive.

Everything is resonant or nothing is. How to be aware of that? We need to find the special resonances that affirm our lives, that make us feel in tune with the way things are.

I am seventeen and away from home, my first year in college. Girls are young women now. One of these lets me see her not as an object but as a fellow creature. This is new! New! We take long, synchronous walks along Lake Michigan singing bebop lines in unison, or trading melodies. I am newborn under a golden sun. Resonance is like that.

I am nineteen, at a Bud Powell concert sponsored by my college jazz club. Bud Powell's plane is late, but his great bassist, Percy Heath, has arrived. The president of the club asks me if I would play piano for a while, accompanied by Mr. Heath, who is all accommodation. Clenching clammy hands I say yes. In public, right then and there, Percy Heath takes me on. His deep certainty becomes part of my own music. I'm riding a wave that comes from the center of the earth. Energies are compounded. My desire and his ability: resonance.

I am twenty-five, the pianist at The Second City Theater in Chicago, forming the habit of practicing every night after hours. During many months of this I learn to recognize the rush of creativity and world love that comes on around 2 A.M. Night resonance.

I am thirty-three, with a lot of music behind me. A North Indian flutist teaches me how to sing a single note in tune, and the fundamental nature of this act occurs to me for the first time. I think, "*Wow,*" and go home to try it by myself. In the privacy of my room I see how many years I've been sleeping. Learning to sing in tune is the first pink in the sky after a restless night of dreams.

Two violoncellos. One leans alone against a wall. You play the other one. The unplayed one sings.

Press down the rightmost piano pedal—it will undampen all the strings. Sing or call; sneeze or bellow; your sound comes back to you in string language.

Broadly speaking, resonance is an answer coming from the unknown, a confirmation of order. It bridges the phenomenal world and the world within, things and their essences, students and teachers, teachers and what is taught. Even its shallow traces confirm meaning and purpose, and give courage; they are a trail of clues in the hunt for beauty.

Speaking more narrowly, resonance depends on periodicity, the evenly spaced vibrations of music. Every physical thing has its natural vibration: the chair its squeak, the pot lid its clang, the guitar its sweet purity. When two strings are tuned to the same pitch their vibrations are synchronized one for one. They are in step, in tune, and each reinforces the other's energy, like the good feeling that arises when you walk in step with your close friend. Resonance, in this sense, is the very core of musical experience.

When you move with music, and sing and play in tune with it, you are feeding its energy, and it is feeding yours. This is the musician's heaven world. As you become more conscious of resonance, that heaven grows wider, more vivid, and more down to earth, where people can use it.

# Walking

I learned about rhythm and meter on late-afternoon walks home from school during my early teens. Since I played the trumpet in the Walnut Hills High School marching band (R. Earl Snapp, director) I knew that the left foot was One and the right foot was Two. During the mile from the end of the bus line to our suburban mailbox, I discovered that left and right is all you need to make a perfect world, yin and yang, the essence of wave, builder of cosmos.

Left, right; boom, chick; down, up; I couldn't get enough. Laden with books, head bent sideways, popping my fingers on the offbeat, I looked like a hipster kid. But I felt like a sleek giant, swaying through the streets. I knew I had hit on a powerful secret, and the experience was ecstasy. That it was hidden inside an everyday activity was as amazing to me then as it is now.

Walking gives permission. When you are walking, the lid is off: the ridiculous boils off into the sublime. It's OK to hum, whistle, sing and shout, clap, snap, beat your body, squint your eyes, dance, jive, swing and sway. Dancers need music, but walkers are their own music.

People walk approximately two steps per second, about 120 steps per minute. Music played at this "walking tempo" makes you feel as though you are walking even if you are sitting down. It resonates with the shape and function of your body. A little faster tempo, a few more beats per minute—say,

130—feels like a brisk walk, pushing it, maybe. Slightly fewer beats per minute—say, 108—feels like a lazy amble, maybe too slow. We are so sensitive to the precise center of this range that conductors use it as a reference point in memorizing various tempi. Everyone knows the feeling of this center; when you know you know it, magic happens.

Take a walk. Enter the rhythm your body gives you. Sing anything. Make up a tuneless tune, or a new language (Legsmouth). Listen to what you are saying in this language; it is a key to your own music. Feel how your breathing and your walking and the sounds you are making modulate one another.

Walking wisdom is natural and lets you learn complex things easily. While keeping your stride free and even, start saying "left, right, left, right" in time with your legs. Then, without altering your gait, accent every third word: "*left*, right, left, *right*, left, right, *left*, right, left, *right*, left, right." This is a basic way of crossing rhythms that has fascinated us unwaveringly for millennia. You'll never get tired of it. Guaranteed. It gives more energy than it takes. You are waltzing and marching simultaneously, balanced between two qualities.

About two-thirds of the way home from school my route ducked between neat houses onto the grounds of the Saint Theresa old folks home and followed along a straight gravel drive, bordered on one side by immense lawns featuring a marble Mother Mary and on the other by a deep maple and sycamore woods sloping down to a creek. The peace of long lives was in the air, and singing, finger-snapping freshman boys had to cool it. It was during this homestretch that the possibility of a world beyond skin and greater than ego might arise, depending on the weather and the light. I remember flickering moments when the two-step cycle and the physical joy it contained would damp down within the late shadows.

Straightening up and looking around, I could see that I was inside a protective green dome of the nature I had come from. The woods and my walking were woven together. The left-right in my rocking body, the pulsing canopy of trees, the histories of ideas in my books, all became a single pulse, *boom-chick*, with many simultaneous frequencies and meanings. I was happy, and overcome by a knowing of wholeness. The two-beat of my walking broke open the mystery of being alive.

Walking is a joiner. It merges the inner and the outer world. Go with it. Listen to the teacher inside it. The lesson is useful, and free.

# Singing with Machines

Pick up the telephone receiver and listen to the dial tone. The sound is nasal, blue-black with silver around the fringes. It is impersonal, the voice of business, a sharp reminder of Yankee ingenuity. It doesn't care about you. It is unwaveringly inhuman, and a great sound to sing against.

Try it. But before you do, put your other hand on the disconnect button so you can momentarily hang up whenever the dial tone needs to be renewed. Snuggle the earpiece up to your ear until the dial tone feels like it is coming from inside your head. Now clear your throat, as if this were an important business call, and sing anything. Sing quietly, balancing the sound of the phone with the sound of your voice. Move your voice around. Hold one pitch and experiment with vowels: *eee* or *aah* or *uuu*. Now match, if you can, the pitch of the dial tone with the pitch of your voice (an octave up for higher voices). Try also to imitate the dial tone's timbre. Your voice will mix well with that internalized quality earphones give. Move your voice up and down slowly to feel out the various harmonic possibilities. It's a duet. Get into it. The dial tone is your slave, your backup group. This could be a natural musical moment before making phone calls. Two or three notes, to remind the machine of its secret nature, keep the faith, give credence to "humming wires."

If your phone is Touch-Tone, dial your own number. You will get a busy signal, but you are now free to play with the buttons without calling New Zealand. Notice that if you start

49

with a corner button and play horizontally you will get one scale, but if you play vertically you will get another. Try the possibilities. Perfect your legato touch until you can move from one tone to the next with no busy signal peeking through. These tones have been especially chosen to be off from the conventional musical scale, so Touch-Tone tunes have their own peculiar character. Of course, no buttons down will give you the rhythmic on-off of the busy signal, an important instrument in your orchestra. Concentrate on what you are hearing. Get serious. Maybe this is the historical imperative of the telephone.

With any luck, your refrigerator makes another good drone, though perhaps more subtle. All electric motors give out a tone that is dependent on the frequency of the AC (alternating current), standardized in the United States at 120 cycles per second, or about B-flat an octave below middle C. Fainter tones are generated as well, making a huge chord. Listen carefully for a moment, then hum along. You're not crazy.

Traffic-light control boxes (the big kind) also give out this electronic chord. Many are the green lights I have awaited singing privately with their drones.

The next time a propeller-driven airplane flies over, listen for how the pitch changes. It will seem to rise as the plane approaches and fall as it disappears. Try to hum the note you hear, or a harmony part. The gradual rise and fall (the Doppler effect) is fascinating when you listen to it. Don't take those everyday airplanes for granted, hear them in a new way, and sing along with what you hear. They can't appreciate the Doppler effect from where they are. Maybe you will discover a new effect and it will be named after you.

"Now she's hummin'," says the auto mechanic after a tune-up. We need to hear machine music. It is an extension of our tolerance, our capacity, our vision of harmonious life.

We need to know that machines don't control us. We need to sing to them in order to recognize that they sing to us. Electrons zipping through wires are neither good nor bad. I have to tell them they are helping me live my life, make my calls, congratulate my Mom, who won a prize at the county fair yesterday for her potpourri.

# Now Time

Lift your arm. Let it fall onto your leg. Simple?

Is existence simple?

Consider that there are two massive objects: the earth—the whole big round rock of it—and your relaxed arm. The reality of the earth's gravitational pull can be experienced in the heavy fall of your arm. Drop your arm again, cosmically this time.

OK, here is a less obvious thought: the mass of your arm is attracting the mass of the earth. Earth-arm force is just as reciprocal as earth-moon force or, in twin stars, star-star force. The earth is falling toward your arm as your arm is falling toward the earth. The attraction is mutual. It's love.

There's a binding force in nature, and gravity is its large-scale expression. Every time you drop your hand, or take a step, or hoe the garden, it is an experience of eternal love. Our bones and the earth are lovers; they embrace when we sleep, they mate when we die.

With a stick, strike a piece of wood. Matter-love. They let loose a brief song. *Thwack.* Matter's love song. The first being who became absorbed in the love song of matter invented music. We keep inventing it every time we play instruments and dance. *Thwack. Boom.* Sticks and bodies falling toward one another, colliding in space. Collision makes everything vibrate. *Conk. Jong. Tunk. Ponk.* Every stroke is a reaffirmation of the love affair, an anniversary card of a never-ending marriage, a moment's "yes." The responsibility of the musician is to feel the yes of every stroke.

You can spend your life practicing this. The most sought-after drummer in Sonoma County, California, is a friend of mine. He is in demand not only because his playing is flashy and energetic but because it is also rock steady. Once I asked him what he practices at home to maintain his excellence. He demonstrated by sitting at his drum set and, with his right foot, playing the pedal (which causes the bass drum to be struck by a large felt mallet) about one beat per second, steady as a metronome, true as time. His eyes fell inward as if in a trance. I had expected exotic percussive fireworks, but there were none. Then I realized that none were needed. There was something about the mix of his perfect concentration and the perfect evenness of the sound, the merging of the stroke and the stroker, the sweet reminder of eternal love as sung by the drum, that was right and sufficient.

He stopped. "That's it?" I asked.

He grinned. "I'll learn it someday."

You can practice this even if you are not the best drummer in your county. Everyone can. All you need is an arm or a stick or a mallet, something it can collide with—your leg, a block of wood, a drum—and the sense that what you are doing is useful because it is connective. Give yourself the authority to do it, to focus your energies on keeping perfect time with a little matter-music.

When time is evenly divided it has a *pulse*. Precise, "metronomic" pulse is a mental construct, like "circle" or "zero" or time itself. Trying to actualize it is stimulating, as is trying to draw a perfectly round circle, or contemplate nothingness, or hear silence. We are tantalized by the impossibility of it. A little lightning comes when we practice the pulse of time.

Here is another way to invite lightning. Imagine for a moment you are trying to collect all your sensibilities, every gleam of your consciousness, into a flash of light called "now."Decide to clap your hands sharply, and call that instant "now." Get ready. Hear everything, see everything. Get set. It will feel like fire. Feel everything. Wide awake, clap your hands, *now*. OK, scatter your brains; then in a moment come back to the practice and do it precisely: *now*. Let your whole self come together in another stroke. *Now*. OK, do this about once every two seconds, gathering energy and then releasing it. Don't give up, even in amazement.

Try gradually increasing the speed to the tempo of vigorous applause. Stop. A little of this goes a long way.

You know that light you saw? Imagine it as a constant beam, with no flicker. Imagine the beings who might be that awake.

# Life Drummer

How else am I going to find out what the world is made of than by thumping and whacking on it, jostling the secret loose with a little loving persuasion? Objects were made to vibrate. There are resonances hidden inside every lump and shard of nature. My nature is to unleash them. I've been doing this to physical bodies since I was an infant—Mama's was the first.

The amazing thing is how drums are an abstraction of mammalian form: skin outside, hollowness inside. Drums are exciting because we make the identification: my own skin stretched over my own hollowness. The body is the first drum. Less obvious are tabletops, ladder rungs, car roofs. When you are a life drummer you learn how everything has its own surface and its own hollowness, and a voice hidden inside waiting for you. Imagine what it's like being locked up for years, maybe generations, in the timbers of a house without having your voice set free. "Please thwack me." Now is your chance. There is work to be done. Make your house happy. "There! No, higher. No, over to the right. Yes! Down an inch. Oh, yes! More. Harder."

Where I practice singing every morning, just behind my head is a beautifully resonant vertical beam set between two floor-to-ceiling windows. If I bang my head backward against it, the whole room reverberates on A-flat in a rich, low octave. Am I crazy to love this dark, round tone coming from my house? My skull thinks it's deep therapy.

Once I lived in a house with stairs so steep I could easily

drum on the steps ahead of me when I walked upstairs. Each board was a pitch in my stair-scale, highly musical carpentry.

I play my dog. He thinks his belly is a drum and his cranium is a gourd and his long snout is a bamboo marimba.

Everything has a sound. Don't be shy. A tap with your finger might reveal a holy book. Take secret pleasure in the fragile sounds of glassware. A life drummer cannot pass a window, a fence, a pole, without knocking or stroking out the sound of it. These tones need to escape, to break out. The voices of metal especially have to be released. Let nothing be safe.

Except the ears of others.

When I was living in my first bachelor apartment, some of my housemates were life drummers like me. We collected metal junk: parts fallen off of cars, organs of dead appliances, broken tools. Someone had even scored the cone-shaped head of a U.S. Navy missile. In the backyard we constructed a jungle-gym rack and hung from it dozens of chunks of vibrant junk. Tire irons were our mallets. It was intense pleasure, once every few days, to go out back and wale away at the metal construction, filling our ears and the neighborhood with ecstatic ringing—the carillon of Middle Earth. Sometimes four or five of us would have an orgy of it.

The problem was that the neighbors were not thrilled. They thought we were making a hideous noise, but we were callous and refused to take the structure down. After a few months of strained relations the novelty wore off. After a few years I recognize how unfair we were to the people who lived around us. This is a confession. My advice: be fair.

I once had a drummer friend who considered his VW bug more interesting as a percussion instrument than as a car. He carried extra pairs of mallets and drumsticks for his friends, and whenever he drove up we played his car, which did not have a square inch of undented surface. This was the right idea, if perhaps extreme.

In liberating sounds, one must be gentle with the physical world and considerate to humans. Mindless drumming is unsociable, as is mindless foot tapping, fingernail clicking, or talking. Though *real* life drummers never pass up an opportunity to unleash the opera of phenomena, they never lose sight of courtesy either.

From the most unlikely sources come the sweetest sounds. Some of them may have been waiting for their freedom. Do your part. The vibrational world needs you. Whack it! Tap it softly and put your ear right up next to it. Or give it a jolt and stand back. Remember, one honors a thing by vibrating it.

THE STUFF OF LIFE DRUMMING

    garbage cans

    plastic buckets

    empty jars and bottles of all descriptions

    boxes, cases, barrels

    metal tanks (like the ones used for propane gas; strike softly
        and listen up close)

    steel bridges

    suspension cables

    metal wires (especially taut ones, but positively nonelectric
        ones)

    stop signs

    toothbrushes on teeth

    screens, grates, anything corrugated

    fence posts

    awnings, tents

    umbrellas, lamp shades

    walls

    air

This list should be endless. Life drummers never rest.

# Dinner Symphony at the Sillses'

Chicago in the early 1960s. We were young musicians and actors and writers discovering the Zen of our lives, or what we called Zen, or the Moment, or the Eternal Now, or I-Thou, depending on whom we were reading, from Watts to Reps to Buber. We were high on the idea of being high on life. It was giddy, to arise in the late, late morning and sense that today might hold some new way of passing through the boundary of ego, some new entering into silence, or life, or others—a greater proof than yesterday's of the interdependence of all things. We didn't talk much about God; mostly we made connections and learned our crafts.

My big discovery was that the sounds of everyday life have a musical nature—their mereness is pleasing and aesthetic if you are receptive. To anyone who would listen, I called attention to the sounds of things, from shoes shuffling to pencils writing. In a restaurant I would be lost in the glassware before the menus arrived.

My upstairs neighbors were Paul and Carol Sills. She was (and is) a painter; he directed The Second City Theater, where I was the musician. One night they invited me for dinner with some mutual friends from work. About ten of us were seated convivially at the round oak table in the kitchen. By the end of the meal, Paul was talking about Buber, as usual, but I was becoming testy about the I-Thou relationship—it wasn't noisy enough for me. I started jiggling with my silverware. Dennis, the stage manager, picked up on the sound and started tapping his wineglass with his fingers. Before long, half a dozen people were playing after-dinner music with their tableware and picked-clean chicken bones, making a respectful accompaniment to Paul's observations. Poised diplomatically between the music and the speech, Carol listened, her features open and expectant. After a moment, with a little laugh, Paul began to accompany himself on pewter pitcher. Now everyone was laughing and making an entertaining little piece. Every combination was tried, several solos, tricky rhythms, innovative timbres.

Suddenly Carol leaps up from the table and searches the cupboards behind her. Meanwhile the piece is peaking and settling down to a gliding finish. As it winds down and threatens to scuttle, Carol reappears, standing at her place with an empty metal ice cube tray in her left hand, a handful of uncooked rice in her right, and a bright gleam in her eye. As she slowly releases the rice into the tray, the pointy little metallic notes fill the space that the other musicians are making for it. Carol's face flushes to debutante pink; her smile has a wild happiness in it. Uncooked rice falling into a metal tray, the finale of a symphony! A stunning idea! Who would have thought?

Then, as all the instruments fade into a final tremolo, Carol tips over the tray in a graceful slow circle around the perimeter of the table. Rice falls on everything, bringing out the most subtle of sounds hidden inside glass, stainless steel, crockery, cloth, and wood. What a masterpiece! What a mess!

Everyone applauded and cheered. We really had made a beautiful connection between sound and music and everyday life and each other. Everyone knew. And Carol's glowing face at the moment of her inspired entrance has been my life model for the way houses are churches, and dinners are symphonies, and earth can be heaven.

# Gibberish

Chicago. A mercury-vapor street lamp shines through the curtains of a child's room. She is two. It is bedtime. She is tucked in and read to. Light out, night-light on. I am torn by love and self-love. Decisions. Goodnight. Leave the door a little open.

Fifteen minutes go by. From her room comes a babbling. I poke my head through the crack in the door. She is sitting up in bed, her covers neatly folded across her lap. Her nightshirt is laundromat wrinkled. Her hands are lying at her sides, palms up, and she is staring with round eyes out to where the opposite wall meets the ceiling. Singsong pours from her. Its highs and lows are modulated with sweet implorings, incontrovertible facts, stern commands, child logic, every vocal gesture she has ever heard from grown-ups. She has the intensity of the deeply convinced. This is the music of language before music or language. With her gaze fixed, her head moves from side to side and her eyes flash. She seems to be in every octave at once. And her face! Her face radiates innocent light, the glow of dawn and newness, the light of born angels. It outshines the street lamp beyond the curtains. And not a word of English is in the waterfall of syllables. Its meaning is light, light turned into sound.

My problems are forgotten. I call her name. "Atha!" She turns to me, her eyes wide and blue. I am the new arrival to her soiree. With a gracious nod of blond curls she continues to babble, but directly to me now. In streams of silvery, musical talk she is telling me of all her lives, her future, her visions, her schemes. She is defending her life with enchantments and spells, filling her room with bright possibility.

I put my arms around her and snuggle her down. She says a half sentence, then a few trailing syllables. In a few seconds she is in a deep sleep.

This wildness of the human tongue is called *glossolalia*, speaking in tongues, and it comes to children or adults in times of great clear channeling. To an observer it gives the impression that the speaker is possessed by an exterior force, but I think it is the speaker who has come into possession of a deep inner spirit. You cannot normally reach this state of exalted babble by willing yourself there. But you can reach beneath everyday language down to the sound that it makes, and to the simple pleasure in the physical operations of speech.

Try, for instance, asking for a glass of water in gibberish. Listen to the strange, unpremeditated language that has leapt from you. Now explain why you are late. Now lie about your finances. Now define love. Now just speak your own brand of gibberish, with no meaning intended, for the fun and the sound of it.

Gibberish reveals the beauty of language, the sheer joy of speech. Be two years old and your present age at once. Have a conversation in gibberish with someone at lunch. Or just say "excuse me" in gibberish to the next person you bump into.

# Say Wind

Say *wind*, but take about five seconds for each letter. Say it smoothly from beginning to end.

You start with slightly pursed lips. Blow some air through. The vocal cords kick in, at first oddly flaccid.

The lips begin to draw back, slightly amused, for the *i*. If you are slow enough you can hear a faint whistle ascending like a stepladder: the overtone series.

Be discriminating about the *i*. Your tongue rises in back. Place the highest part of it just so—there is a pure vowel in there.

Now the tip of the tongue begins to curl up to touch the hard palate directly behind the front teeth, choking off the vowel.

As you say *n* you are breathing through your nose, and the bones in the front of your face are vibrating like a viola.

Magic moment: the tip of the tongue flexes ever so slightly at the instant the vocal cords disengage; it sounds like *d*.

A last eddy of breath pushes out: escaped wind.

Now say *window*.

Now say *window washer*. Go slow. Slower.

If you look in the encyclopedia (or a big dictionary) under "International Phonetic Alphabet" you will see a fascinating chart of phonemes, the basic sounds of speech, arranged according to the anatomy of our speech organs. The consonants are shown essentially from front-formed to back-formed, which means from lips to glottis. Say *pin, tin, key, cod, chutzpa.* The initial consonants of these words progress from the front of the lips to the back of the throat, the vellum. You can go farther by making a voiceless catch in your glottis. Now say the initial sounds only, leaving off the rest of the words so there is no vocalization whatever—six consonants that progress smoothly from lips to glottis. Practice the series slowly until you can do it fast, all six in two seconds or less. Experience the intelligence of your muscles. The fundamental sounds of speech are organized by body wisdom, brought back home.

Try saying *think, then, sing, zero.* Again, leave off the ends of the words, but this time include the voiced beginning of each vowel. In this sequence, the tip of the tongue moves from a forward position (between the teeth) to curled back. In the symbols of the International Phonetic Alphabet it looks like this: θ ð s z. Spoken as a single word it is one of the Ten Thousand Most Beautiful Sounds.

The vowels are amazing. Say *keen, fit, fate, care, sang, ask, father, dog, jaw, go, full, rule.* Now drop out all the consonants and slowly elide the twelve vowels together so as to make one smooth spectrum of changing sound. Try it backward, then forward. Now do this without changing the pitch of your voice. Many times, slow. Listen deep. If you think you've heard it, you haven't. In one way, no sound could be more natural to us. Yet there is more complexity here, more unmined beauty, than ever meets the ear.

Diphthongs are arcs of this circle of vowels. *Pout,* for instance, moves forward from *ask* (approximately) to *rule. I,* astonishingly, moves backward from *father* to *keen.* To check this out, prepare to say *I,* but vocalize only the first one-hundredth of a second of the first sound: you will find yourself set to pronounce the *a* of *father.* Slow down the diphthong sufficiently and you will hear the gradations between the pure vowels.

My Hungarian grandmother couldn't say the *th* of *mouth.*

She said *mout*, with a hard *t*. We kids would try to get her to put her tongue between her teeth and grunt, but she would weep from embarrassment and anger. Then she would say, "Big mouts! You tink you know everyting," and we would lose it. It was funny then. My regrets are thirty years too late.

We listen to foreigners, wondering why they cannot speak like we do. Who knows what exquisite things we cannot say, or even hear correctly? There is such a heap of wondrous sound in our mouths, waiting to be heard.

Universal as it is, not many people know about the International Phonetic Alphabet. It has allowed me to hear languages more clearly, my own and foreign ones as well. It has set me closer to the vibrational source of it all.

Take nothing for granted, not even the mother tongue that is part of your flesh. Relearn to talk, even if you spend only two minutes trying. You will see that there is a joy in it; in plain daily talk there is a playful joy.

# Chanting

Think of all the ways we have contrived to chant collectively. Sports, opera, prayer, children's games, political action. Famous chants:

Go!
Sweep!
Balk!
Bravo!
Brava!
Encore!
We want lunch!
Two, four, six, eight,
    Who do we appreciate?
    Norwood, Norwood!
Hell, no, we won't go!
Om
Allah-hu
Ram

When the need for collective expression arises, a chant usually arises along with it. The words seem to appear by consensus, the sound of collective intention.

Less easy to describe is what happens when you chant alone. It is a way of experiencing privately what we have all experienced socially. One chants not with other people but with aspects of oneself. Or perhaps there are other souls one senses. Or an oversoul, a guiding spirit. In this mode, chanting is invocatory—it tunes you in with what is more than you and calls that aspect forward.

I use chanting to hollow out my ears and my heart, as a prayer for capacity. The two best chants I know are *sa* and *om*. Neither has primarily denotive meaning; their meaning is the sound they make. *Sa* is the beginning note of the musical scale. It comes from Sanskrit and is used in Indian music. The note that has its name is intended to be the foundation of something. When sung it makes an open sound, and wins hands down over the *do* of *do re mi*. It is a world and it implies a world.

*Om*, or *aum*, goes slowly through a wide spectrum of vowels and ends with a hum through your nose. You swing through an arc of change and learn to feel motionless inside that change. Both *sa* and *om* are meant to bring you into the present, into the act of making the sounds themselves, with their boundless intricacy, as well as into the simplicity of the gesture. But there are other possibilities you can make up, or find in spiritual practices from numerous sources. Try *yo*, or *wa*, or *hu*, or any sound that will genuinely absorb your interest over several long minutes. If it sounds good to you, chances are it means "God" or "thanks" or "please rain" in some language.

Find a quiet spot, become quiet, decide on a syllable or two, observe your breath going in and out a few times. Then, on the next out breath, vocalize the chant, not loudly. Let it settle down as much as possible onto a single sustained pitch, the same pitch with every repetition. The idea is to make it more and more the same each time, while noticing more and more about it. If thoughts come, let them float on the sound. Enter into the sound of the sound. Be breathed by your breathing. Pictures will come and go, maybe a whole movie, yet each next breath is a chance for a new, perfect absorption. Eventually the screen clears. You will hear your own overtones at the fringes, like a rainbow. Now see the sound as translucent: where does the light that filters through it come from? Speed up or slow down slightly, and lengthen or shorten the sound, so as to keep your metabolic balance. Quit when you're ahead.

Or, as a more formal alternative, give yourself exactly three minutes. Or five minutes. Or, even better, eleven breaths, or twenty-one, or thirty-three.

# Willing Silence

There is no such thing as pure silence, not in the world we know. Pure silence is an ideal, an infinite quality like "emptiness" or "perfection." We can think about it. We can approach it more and more closely and feel its pull. But as an experiential reality it is impossible—impossible because we are alive. Our body of blood and breath is a raucous machine. Our very ears produce sound, or the clear sensation of it. Existence itself is full of noisy energy, not empty anywhere. A recent issue of *Science News* refers to a vacuum as "a seething sea of electromagnetic fields . . . a giant reservoir into which excited atoms can deposit photons."[1]

And yet we do experience what can be called relative quiet, the impression of silence, and this can be vivid and compelling. We are drawn toward it. We are hungry for it and it nourishes us. In a brief moment of quiet sitting we can realize how tranquillity is the precondition for listening. Our sense of silence is the other side of our sense of sound, and gives definition and wholeness to it. It is the touchstone, the gut check which triggers creativity.

If we cannot directly experience pure silence, we can experience our longing for the ideal it represents, just as we can experience our longing for the ideal of perfection. It is in this quality of longing that the ideal of silence becomes useful as a practice, a very musical practice. We can learn to stimulate the longing, to will it to the front, to feel it even in the midst of sound. Author and piano tuner Anita T. Sullivan says that we experience it, when we tune our instruments, as "a place in the center of all the pronged tremblings. . . . like silence would be if we could hear it, but of course we cannot. . . . You have stopped hearing with just your ears. You have stopped. And then, I think, you fall the rest of the way in, to the unison. . . . there is an area where you cross—suddenly—and there you *are*. You can never know what happened on the way over because you were falling."[2]

One evening in 1985 I was playing a solo piano concert in San Francisco. I was in the middle of a long improvisation when the ceiling opened up and there was the head of my spiritual teacher Murshid Sam Lewis—who died in 1971—smiling down at me. He was enveloped in silver light and looked like the Sistine chapel. After an interval of communion I realized that even though I was playing the piano there was no sound. We were in a heaven world of perfect silence. I said, "Murshid, I have to go now, I'm playing a concert." Zoop! the ceiling closed like a curtain, and I was back in E major again.

I think, if you do your silence homework, the ideal of silence will come close to you in unexpected moments. When you bend your will toward silence you will find the effort life-giving. "When you look for God," says Rumi, "God is in the look of your eyes."[3] Willing yourself toward silence is the quintessential practice, the springboard for music. You can do a swan dive from it and enter directly into your work without making a sound.

# PRACTICING

# Finding Your Own Music

Some people have fear about improvising their own music. They have invested so much time and care in playing music that has been composed by someone else—usually a dead someone else, like Bach or Ravel—that there doesn't seem to be any way of leaving the printed page.

On the other end of the spectrum are the folks who avoid playing anything that sounds like anyone else; they need to feel original, to reaffirm in each note their personal freedom. There is a dread of being cliché, hackneyed, trapped by the culture: "It's been done before."

Actually, all music is village music. We are collective beasts, more collective than individual. Our music reflects this. Even artists who seem to jut out angularly from their culture, like Beethoven or Cecil Taylor, are speaking for their village, though their village may be hard to find. Maybe theirs is a village of some particular mind set, a prevalent psychology, an ephemeral community of feeling. Even if their village seems crazy to us, or irresponsible, or suicidal, it nevertheless exists, just beyond the trees.

On Bali there are villages where almost everyone carves or paints or weaves or plays music or dances. Though some individuals obviously excel, it is embarrassing to be better than someone else. The communal flow is highly valued; special talent is scarcely noticed. Too much recognition rocks the boat. Over the generations, Balinese art has become refined and extraordinarily powerful, but the contribution of individual artists is blended in very gradually.

So the very idea of "finding your own music" is in some ways counter to culture. Yet there are millions of us "looking for our own music." That's *our* village.

The truth is, the line between what is uniquely yours and what is given to you by your culture is invisible to you. Don't worry about it. Your village is inside you. Your work is to go inside and bring out the sounds you like to hear. There is a sense of value inside you that is more powerful than either your individual self or your cultural self. And there are music practices that can lead you to that sense, and teach you how to hook into it, live inside it, and eventually express it to the assemblage of villages.

If you enter sound deeply enough, you break open into that world, the soul world where universal music comes from. From that world a shakuhachi flute player plays, and Bulgarian women sing love songs. That village is the same village everyone is from. The gift of sound is that it guides your steps to that place.

# One Note after Another

When you enter sound you will find your own music there. The best practice I know for entering sound is to play "One Note after Another" on your instrument (on your voice if you sing). I'll describe the exercise first as if played on the piano. But everyone can do this, even those who have never learned an instrument.

You need a quiet room.

The practice starts out like "Listening to a String," which means, in this case, striking a key and holding it down. Any key will do, though the ones more or less in the middle of the keyboard are best to begin with. As you hold the key down, listen intently to the note thus produced. Immerse yourself in the ray of sound as though it were the light of a landscape. Get lost in it. Scrutinize every detail, memorize the terrain through telescope and microscope. Relish the play of light as the tone decays. When you have heard at your maximum capacity, strike another midrange key and open the door wider. When you have heard all you can hear, strike another, and so on until the experience is reliable.

You will begin to recognize a certain moment when you've *got* the note, a little nod inside the ear when you have registered its essence: *Yes, I'm hearing it.* The cup is more full than empty. At the nod, you are free to choose another note. The remarkable thing is that the nod may come at any time during the life of the note—after twenty seconds or after a fraction of a second. But there will be a moment when your sense of fullness gives you permission to go on to the next note.

There is an enormous trick inside this exercise. Although it begins as a concentration on individual notes, a connection between notes gradually emerges. The nature of the connection deserves our attention. When the game is well played, you do not consciously choose the new note; there is no right or wrong. The unconscious does it, with impunity. No value is placed on how the pitches relate up and down, that is to say, their melodic content. Yet, after being filled with one tone, the desire for a lower one, or a higher one, or a much lower or higher one, or even the same one, arises. It arises not through the intention of carving out a melody but through the pleasure of filling up the whole space with sound, much like filling a canvas with paint as opposed to painting a picture. If you find yourself trying to make a melody, stop. Go back to being filled up with individual tones. Let the melody make itself, let the sounds choose the sounds. Don't worry, you'll be part of the choice. But the part of you that is in the mix is not your mind; it is your response to total absorption in tone.

When you practice this over several days you learn to ride easy in the saddle. Your absorption in sound works like a trusty mule beneath you and a path of music emerges, one note after another.

Even then, it is hard to maintain the purity of the intuitive stream. Why? Because we are seduced by the mind. We begin to hear the melodies that *are* coming out, our intellect takes over, we start sculpting, making Art. "Don't be seduced by the melody!" I bellow at my students, "listen to the sound." But really it is OK—go ahead and be seduced. It's only love, and the game lovers play.

This simple practice allows you to be in the womb where

melodies gestate, the deep space previous to mind. Whenever I improvise, especially in public, I begin with this pure music. The intellect will rev up soon enough; but you have to bring the soul in from note one.

# Telephoning Counts

At first, the idea of practicing music comes from afar, like the idea of going to the subtropics, or getting married, or building your own house. Little events might bring you closer to the big event—a chance musical workout with fortunate results, or a close encounter with an inspiring musician. But a wide river of work separates the sensitive listener who does not practice from the one who does. The river is crossed, in time. It may take years to form the practicing habit. But the length of time does not matter. The important thing is to allow the impulse to root and blossom in its own natural growing cycle.

There are things you can do to nurture the process. One is to make an altar, but not a physical one—a temporal one. Reserving a place in your daily schedule gives practicing a time to happen. Five or ten minutes may be enough, a half hour may be a lot. Eventually your practice time becomes a bright corner of your day, a haven, a meeting with a friend who gives you stuff you didn't have before.

Clearing the forest is part of building the house. It takes a lot of energy to clear a little bit of land. Maybe it will take forty minutes to clear thirty minutes of practice time. You may have to telephone someone to drive the kids, or watch someone else's kids in return for them watching yours, or change a meeting. You may have to make some coffee to get wired, or read the funnies to calm down. These preliminaries are part of the practice process, part of the flowering into music, part of the music. Even telephoning counts. When you are dialing the number of the baby-sitter you can say to yourself, "I'm doing music now."

# The Ace of Practice

Getting yourself to practice regularly is like getting yourself to floss your teeth, or write your folks regularly, or meditate. Music is such a private part of us, it touches us in so deep and vulnerable a place, that evasion of practice can seem quite reasonable: Why disturb what is sleeping so deeply? Why mess with a functional inertia?

In reply to these dissuasions you have an ace up your sleeve. Here is how to play it: Make a no-nonsense deal with yourself to write down—the night before—the time you intend to practice the next day, and for how long. For instance, on Tuesday evening write, "Wed. 2:00—twenty minutes." It takes a few seconds to do that. Write it in a book you carry with you or on a piece of paper that stays in one place. Be sure you see it the next morning so it can be a target. If you don't practice at the specified time, try for later. If you miss, don't beat yourself up. So you missed. At least you wrote it down.

The deal is not to practice, but to commit to paper, without fail, your intention to practice. Even if you have to write, "Wed. 2:00—ten seconds," do that. It accomplishes two things: It makes it easier to practice. It also gives you an objective look at the person who thinks he wants to practice. Maybe you should not be practicing music in the first place. It is not for everyone, not every last one of us. But if you are flirting with the idea of practice, it means that something is tugging at you under the surface, something worth investigating, worth making a breathing hole for. If music practice turns out to be your work to do, this method will help you get closer to it.

# Cosmic Practice

The more your music practice becomes regular, the more real it feels and the more it pays off. Music itself depends on regularly recurring cycles, on periodicity, such as the vibrations of strings and reeds. Consider how the daily rotation of the earth, the monthly orbit of the moon, and their yearly orbit of the sun are also periodic. These motions make a kind of slow-moving music, too deep for our ears. But we sense the music of the spheres because it was the condition of our origin. We are made from this music.

When you practice every day, you come into resonance with cosmic cycles. After many days you can feel the diurnal cycle inside your work; after many moons, the lunar; after years and years the constellations come in. The whole spectrum of vibration, from the slow, lowest tones of turning galaxies to the highest speeds of inner light, becomes your musical realm.

# Ima Dork

The practice of music can push every button you have, especially the one that puts yourself down. Sometimes I think my mantra is Ima Dork. It, or one of its angry cousins, will pierce a seamless period of concentration, mixing self-denial in with the pure tones. Working musicians confess every variation on this theme.

When we practice, the ideal of beauty is held close. We attempt precise psychological expressions and exacting physical motions. When the music we actually play is off the idealized mark, we become supercritical and toss it, and ourselves along with it.

We want to be beautiful and creative, and we continually refer to cultural models who are supposed to be. We do fear the failure of not living up to these standards of success. Not having the right stuff is the American nightmare. When we seem to lack our quota of power or ability we get scared, and from this fear comes self-anger.

This is a deep problem and I don't know the solution. But I do know that music can be learned only one way: by absorption in vibration. A mind immersed in the sound of sound does not have room for angry captions. When you hear that disparaging critic, don't try to shut it up, because it can outtalk you. Slow down; take a breath, stand up, turn around, shake hands with the good energy in your striving, then fight vinegar with honey. Zero in on the sweet sound of musical sound. Your self-nagger may seem all consuming and out of control, but musical tone has greater power than even that voice.

# In Meter

Walking is the most natural measure of time. Walking tempo—about two beats per second—is a reference tempo for music because it feels central to human life. Singing, chanting, making percussionlike noises, or playing with rhythmic language while walking is one of the great joys. This can be a private pleasure or one you share with other walkers.

Someday I want to be in a walking choir. Hardly anyone will be able to hear us except ourselves and a few astonished passersby. We will march down farming roads and through bedroom communities, stomp across malls and over bridges. We will tramp through industrial parks. "Did you hear that, Harold, sounded like a giant kazoo?" We will sing a little Beach Boys and a little Bach and a lot of gospel. The Overland Singers. The Walking Gospel. Doctor Walker and the Troops. No instruments, not even megaphones; just throats and feet and some banners blowing. We'll need some good sun hats, too. During the long stretches between towns we'll improvise never-before-and-never-again vocal symphonies for the marathon bicyclists and the cows.

The good vibrations of walking and dancing need to be internalized, then brought thoughtfully into practice. Tap a foot in walking tempo, and play a one-note piece inside that meter. The truth about playing in time is so simple that most folks can't believe it. It is this: when you become totally absorbed in the "now, now, now, now" of walking tempo, the music will structure itself. You hardly have to think about the music—in fact, try not thinking about it at all. Just concentrate on the beat and listen attentively to what comes out. Do not let yourself take the beat for granted, like you do the rooms in your house, even for a millisecond.

At first you may be playing one note per foot tap. Then new notes will appear in various rhythms—you are acquiring new furniture and moving it around in the rooms. But remember that in this exercise the pulse is fundamental, and the moment you've lost the "now" of it you've lost the meaning of it. Put your heart in the simplicity of it, in the joyous, unending periodicity of it, and whole, strong music will emerge.

You may discover that you do not have to play a note on every beat, that it is good to rest during certain ones and to skirt on either side of others. Try avoiding the beat, then playing on it. Playing off the beat and on the beat is the yin and yang of musical time. Both are needed for music to feel complete. Concentrating on this is like being conscious of your own metabolic cycles, but from inside of them, where they are single-minded and faithful.

Let walking tempo be your first reference, then try faster speeds and slower ones.

Walking meter naturally groups into two complementary beats: left, right; or boom, chick. That is duple meter. Now try triple meter—waltz time: boom, chick, chick, boom, chick, chick (evenly spaced). Improvise music inside of *that* house. Virtually all of music everywhere is some combination of, or alternation between, duple and triple meter. It is another case—an astounding one—of complex results from simple structures.

Meter is so compelling that even the best musicians have to remind themselves, when locked in the swing and sway of it, to remember the other dimensions: loud and soft, staccato and legato, rough, smooth, cajoling, majestic, peaceful.

When you feel comfortable playing in duple and triple meters, try deliberately playing without any underlying pulse—outside the house, where time is wind. Then play in meter again and know the difference between the measured and unmeasured realms. Now without it again, and savor that difference.

# Disabusable Notions

## 1. *I'm not musical*
## (Alternate: *I'll never be any good anyway*)

What is true is that you are not *as* musical as _____ (fill in the blank with someone more musical than you, from J.S. Bach to Aretha Franklin).

The purpose of music is for you to become who you are, to bring what is inside you into play, to spin a vibrating thread through the world, to spark life. Music is everyone's birthright, and everyone who wants to can claim it. There will always be someone more musical than you; but there is always more music in you to uncover—more pitches, more rhythms, a finer sense of proportion, a clearer perception of your aural world. I have never seen a person who said of their breath, "That is someone else's breath," or a person who did not recognize the music in their own soul once it was shown to them. Even if other people have told you the opposite, the day you claim your innate music is a musical day for the whole world.

## 2. *You have to learn other people's music before you learn your own*

Music does not belong to individuals so much as it belongs to cultures and to humanity. When you learn other people's (or peoples') music you *are* learning your own, and when you are discovering your own you are discovering everyone's. The important thing is to learn music, yours and others', or anywhere in between. There is no official map through this territory. Learn what interests you first, and your range of interest will increase.

### 3. *Music from the rest of the world isn't as advanced as ours*

We have, after all, Mozart, Stravinsky, Charlie Parker, et al. These musicians are our cultural mirrors, and in them we recognize the best in ourselves. Yet the richest values of each culture are reflected in its music. The condition of the soul is as clearly perceived through the best of African music, or the best Hindi music, as it is through Bach. High beings are high beings; good music is good music.

There is no arguing this point. It has to be heard. If you haven't heard it and you are interested, listen to some of the best music from other cultures as if it were you yourself making that music. As you open to those masters you will appreciate even more the music from home, and your own music will grow in proportion.

It is clear, incidentally, that certain cultures specialize in the development of certain aspects of music. Sixteenth- and seventeenth-century Europe had counterpoint covered. Africa has cross rhythms down. India is the one for melodic line. But no one owns the highest part, the soul connection. That belongs to everyone equally.

# The Best Excuses

*I don't feel like it.* Anything that requires uninterrupted consciousness seems like work. When we are actually *practicing* consciousness, like meditation or music, it feels like good work that does itself. But when we are inactive, there is an anxiety around it. Inertia is our defense. "My legs are too heavy." "My brain is too thick." "I'm comfortable where I am." We feel our resistance as though it were a natural state. At the self who says, "Go ahead and do it—it feels good," we look sideways.

My advice: Whether or not you actually practice, spend some time hanging out with your resistance—especially if it is strong. Peer deeply at the face beneath the face, as though you were reading the mind of an ape at the zoo. Then at least you will recognize "I don't feel like it" as a cover for deeper feelings. Opening that window might be considered your music practice for the day.

*I'm not inspired.* Musicians are not angels. Most of our work is down here on earth with earthly objects: strings, skins, reeds, fingers, lips, and legs. We huff and pluck. Our faces get red and our muscles get tired. Forget inspiration. Music is sweat-hog work. Sometimes inspiration does come, with clear round eyes, as though she had never been away; if we have been toiling we are ready to receive her. Pound and blow the physical world until it rings and warbles. Be the master of that. Then when the muse does arrive she will appreciate your preparations and linger over tea, perhaps well into the evening.

*But everybody's listening.* It's a creepy feeling when you think the neighbors upstairs are listening to every note you are playing. And the people passing by in the street. And your partner. Your skull is full of their observations. "That was a dumb move." "Not so loud." "Slow down." "Why don't you give up and go on to something else?" "You heart's not in it." "It was better yesterday."

You answer this stream with your own. "I hope they appreciate how sensitive my soft notes are. Good chord. They should send over dessert for the trill. You've got to admit this is better than it was three months ago. These are *sixty-fourth* notes." More darkly: "I know they are tired of this. They should move if they don't like it. Oops, *that* mistake. Sorry. Oops, sorry again. Oh well, I'll practice another part. I know you hate this. Would D minor be better? Maybe I should play something I know. I'm such a *beginner*."

Or, most perniciously, with the image of your teacher floating in your retina, "I made this up myself. Watch this: perfect control. Is it too slow? Don't be angry. Go away. Please don't go away. How was that? I did what you told me. C *minus*? Could you raise it to a B for my mom? Listen to this scale. Oops, sorry again . . ."

So everybody's listening except you. They are listening to your music and you are listening to them. If you are practicing within your rightful territory, their listening is likely to be in your imagination. The chatter you hear is really your own chatter.

When you practice, practice for you. When you daydream about what others hear, you miss the essence of your labor. Build a protected zone of concentration around yourself, with the sound of your music as the wall. Listen more keenly and forgivingly to your work, and leave others to do their own work. Be an audience of one. This results in higher standards and is best for everyone in the long run.

# Mistakes

We ordinarily use mistakes to fuel self-denial, as a proof of our incompetence. But since mistakes are inevitable, try turning them instead to your best advantage. Embrace your mistakes; accept the self who makes them. This is the creative response, one that allows music to find its true shape inside you.

Mistakes are your best friends. They bring a message. They tell you what to do next and light the way. They come about because you have not understood something, or have learned something incompletely. They tell you that you are moving too fast, or looking in the wrong direction.

Mistakes might be detailed instructions on how to take apart and rewire physical motions, muscle by muscle. Or they might show you where you have not heard clearly, where you have to open up the music and listen again in a new way. Examine a mistake as if you had found a rare stone. Run over the edges of it with your tongue. Peer inside the cracks of it. Hold it up to the sun, turning it a little this way and that. When you have learned what you can from it, toss it away casually, as if you didn't expect to see it again. If it shows up later, be patient and polite, and make a new accommodation. A mistake knows when it isn't needed, and eventually will leave for good.

The goal is not to make music free of mistakes. The goal is to be complete in learning, and to grow well.

# Wandering Mind

Learning to concentrate is like drawing a picture of your hand drawing a picture of your hand. Or describing the act of describing.

In such pursuits one's capacity seems to increase and decrease unpredictably. The important thing is to remember what you are doing, which is concentrating.

Maybe seeing a movie of yourself slouched all over the furniture will supply the objectivity needed to remind you to sit up straight. But how are you going to take a movie of the quail in your mind?

Try this. Ask a friend, a *good* friend, or a trusted teacher, to help you. Sit the person down and begin to improvise *very* simple music. Commit yourself totally to being inside the sound. Concentrate. At the first intrusion of thought, stop the music and verbalize the thought. The music may last for only one note, then, "This is really dumb." Another note, then, "I forgot to pay the car insurance and I'm out of stamps." Take a deep breath, renew your intention, and play for perhaps five whole seconds before, "Christine was wearing a truly ugly dress, but she was so adorable for buying me lunch."

Continue to do this for a few minutes—enough to get an idea, through your friend's witness, of your mind's delight in wandering. It may be vexing to turn your mind inside out like this, but it is funny, too. So laugh a lot. The next time you sit down to play, you might be closer to holding those fluttering little birds in your warm hands.

# No One Can Tell You

Nothing is as private as the place inside you that responds to music. That place belongs to you. You are the boss of it, and the carpenter, and the janitor also. No one else can qualify what goes on in there. No one can tell you that a chord is sad or dissonant, or that a progression is unresolved, or that a passage is purple. You have to hear that for yourself. A thing is not true unless it is true for you.

Nor can anyone tell you what is good or bad, what to like or not like. If you adore a piece of corny music, then corn is good to eat. (I cry at movies.) If you don't like Bach, that is Bach's loss. There is no need to feel defensive about your responses. If a piece appeals to you, for you that music is good. If it sounds good it *is* good.

When you are working out your own music, strip down what you hear to its vibrational essence. If you like it, keep it. If you want to change it, change it. If you want to throw it away, bye-bye. In this work you are the one who ultimately decides, not your teachers, not your culture, not the shadowy opinions of others. You must be devoted to what sounds good in your center.

More often than not, as I was learning my own musical language, I would hear my teacher's voice say, "I don't like that," or, "I approve." Or my own worried voice: "People will think that is too bland" or "too rough," or "That will bore them." It took years to hear the sound of the music louder, fuller, and truer than those voices. I still have to remind myself constantly: only the music can tell you.

# What Should I Practice?

It doesn't matter what you practice as long as your energy for it is hot. It is the quality of your practice that matters, just as it is the quality of your love that matters, not whom you love. If you are hearing ragtime with special clarity this week, practice ragtime. If it is time to improvise, then improvising is your practice. If all you really want today is to listen to Ravel, listen. If you are really doing it, it doesn't much matter what you do. But "really" means *really*, which means absolute absorption, no veils.

The secret of "really" is to keep track of what you actually do practice, not as a policeman but as an anthropologist. Simply log your cycles of interest. On a piece of graph paper, let the vertical axis be a list of your projects, let the horizontal axis represent days. Filling in a square means you have done a complete job (however you define it) on that project for that day. You can fill in half a square, or shade it, or put a little dot there to show you thought about it. After a month you see a reflection of your work in music. It is a mirror that lets you see part of your life.

My guidelines to students are: spend about a quarter of your practice time on other people's music (Bach, Monk), a quarter on theory and technique, a quarter improvising or composing, and a quarter listening. This is different for each person and each day. The important thing is to develop the arrow of intuition. When a certain technical skill is required to achieve a certain sound you want, you will *want* to practice that technique. The want for sound comes first, then the want for technique. There is no ought in it. "Practice whatever you want" requires consciousness of your want. Music is deep work.

It is valuable to have many pots on many burners, and to keep track of the pots and the fires under them. This means that it is good to nurture diverse musical interests with well-defined, coherent projects in which to develop them. Be practicing and listening to several kinds of music at once; have diverging creative directions. On any given day, go for whatever is cooking best—stir that pot. One's interest boils and cools unpredictably. Don't hassle it. Be responsive to your muse, not controlling. Do what she says. Coherence will come over time.

The secret of coherence is to keep an updated list of your interests and projects in a precious book that is always near you. This list is your sober overview. It lets you see all your musical aspirations at a glance and gives you a feel for how you are moving through your musical life.

# Technique and the Eraser Trick

To the astonishment of my students, I grab hold of two pencils, one in each fist. With the eraser ends I improvise a piece on the piano: cascades of notes; soaring melodies; gripping harmonies. They can't believe it. I have played a complex piece essentially with my wrists and two stumps of rubber.

How do I do that?

All modesty aside, I know which notes to play. I know what I am hearing, and where to find the corresponding notes on the keyboard.

Obviously, one can always use more technique. I surely could, despite the arduous years of working for what I have. The farther along you are in music the more motivated you are to practice for speed, strength, and precision. But technique is rarely your limit. The weak link is the ear. What is truly needed is to hear more deeply and to know more precisely where you are on the coordinates of musical space and time. When you can play what you hear, you will know naturally what technique to practice, and you will want to. This is where a teacher sensitive to your personal search can be most helpful.

But sound is the first teacher. Let it be what guides you, not the *idea* of being a brilliant player.

# Electronic Instruments

I am not a fan of electronic instruments, by which I mean synthesizers and samplers. It's not that I don't like them— sometimes I do. It's just that when you listen deeply to an acoustic instrument you hear wood, breath, the fibers of cane. When you listen deeply to electronic music, you hear electrons. I like electrons. But I *love* wood, breath, reeds, skin, and hair. These I can identify with when I make love, or walk along the beach, or think. Yes, I know I am *made* of electrons, that they are what moves in me, especially in the neural paths connecting my ears to my brain. But they are infrastructure, not objects of desire. They are what I hear *with*, not what I want to hear.

Actually, making love with electrons is fascinating, but not for long. So my threshold for electronic music, and even recorded or amplified music, is low. There is just no substitute for living flesh. The sounds of organic things can be simulated, and the simulation decorated with eleven dimensions, but you will sooner or later find your way back to the wooden flute you packed in straw for safekeeping.

This is my personal bias. People must follow their loves and needs. It is true that the infant electronics industry, now bawling for the instant gratification of its consumers, is fast maturing. Increasingly, it will become possible to make truly strong and beautiful music on electronic instruments. Even now, synthesizers do introduce people to a new realm of sound in an immediate way.

Please. If you spend a lot of time with electronic instruments, balance that experience with acoustic ones, with the vibrations of metal and plants and animals, and with your own voice of flesh and breath.

# Deep Pantry

Keep track of all your musical ideas that work, as well as the plain ones that show only faint promise. Record them in any medium: musical notation, tape, computer memory, hieroglyphics of your own devising. Date what you record—make a sort of musical diary—and review it from time to time. As long as you have a retrieval system, the creative material in your dormant memory interpenetrates and nourishes itself. An old idea languishing in the pantry grows little shoots and connects to other ideas in ways it could not imagine when it was a seedling.

Such a cache doesn't accrue by itself. It takes discipline, the coherent kind, arcing over months and years. But the process will nudge you toward your own distinctive and genuine musical style. The closest thing to a free lunch is coming across a forgotten fragment that makes you happy. "I was just a kid when I wrote that a year ago, but, hey, the kid was all right!"

Also, don't stay too long with things that *are* working. Too quickly they can become formulas and hold you back from searching and being hungry. The best thing for a bright idea threatening to become a cliché is a long nap in the pantry for some nourishing darkness.

# Lentus Celer Est

This is bogus Latin for Slow (lentils) Is Fast (celery). Write it large somewhere. It means you cannot achieve speed by speedy practice. The only way to get fast is to be deep, wide awake, and slow. When you habitually zip through your music, your ears are crystallizing in sloppiness. It is OK to check your progress with an occasional sprint. But it is better to let speed simply come on as a result of methodical nurturing, as with a lovingly built racing car.

Yet almost everyone practices too fast, their own music as well as others'. We want to be the person who is brilliant. This desire is compelling, and it can become what our music is about.

Pray to Saint Lentus for release from zealous celerity. Pray for the patience of a stonecutter. Pray to understand that speed is one of those things you have to give up—like love—before it comes flying to you through the back window.

# Names

Most musicians can name some of the elements in their music. A few can name everything nameable. The rest of us fall somewhere in between, able to name certain things and without the foggiest idea about others. No musician, of course, chooses to be naming the events in a piece while actually performing it. To the extent that you are describing an experience, you are not really having it. So why go to the trouble of naming musical things in the first place?

Names allow the intellect to grab hold of material and structure it. They allow us, during our periods of practice and contemplation, to categorize points on the graph of musical space and time, and organize them into a grammar and syntax that conveys meaning. The structure of a symphony or a fugue is partially a result of this discipline, as is an intelligent improvisation.

But not all music emphasizes such structure. The most deeply felt music—a lullaby or a prayer or a song of jubilation—can have the simplest organization. This is not to say that there is no mind in such music, nor feeling in a fugue. Every music has its appropriate mixture.

A shepherd alone on a hill needs only to be tuned to nature for his music to please sheep, man, and God. Part of us wants to be that shepherd. But we have lost him, we and Adam. Our intellects have been pricked, we have been brokered into the world of names; our innocence is long gone. We have become our hungry minds. That is why some of us have the guilty feeling we should be learning music theory: we hear our minds clamoring to be used. Meanwhile, the other part of us wants to sit on the hill in vasty namelessness, playing the eternal flute.

The blessing: in music practice, the mind and the heart learn to relate in graceful proportion. They open to one another and memorize each other's ways. They make love and they bargain. If your heart is eclipsed when you are making music, your music will leave you cold; this is a signal to open the gate of feeling. If your mind is restless, your music will bore you; this is a signal for you to learn musical grammar, so more of your intellect will come into play.

You are somewhere between a shepherd's song and a grand fugue—no one can tell you where. A book cannot tell you. Listen openly to your own music as it develops. It will tell you what is needed for the perfect mixture of mind and heart.

# Chariot of Words

The secret to setting words to music is to say the words and to hear the words you are saying as if they were music. Songwriters usually construct songs from exaggerations of the contours and accents of speech. (Obversely, some lyricists hear words of heightened meaning hidden inside a melody.)

If you write poems, or lyrics, or lyrical prose, and you want to set your words to music, first say the lines you write and then sing them as an extension of your patterns of speech, even if this seems awkward or silly. Proceed line by line, taking the time to refine each phrase. Then use a tape recorder, or your instrument, or both, to bring you closer to a musical expression.

It is good to start with short poems of just a few syllables, like haiku. There is no immediate need for rhyme, or anything complex or forced. If the words are real for you, you will discover their music. In most cultures, poetry without music is just plain nudity.

Set a few words of your own to a phrase of original music. Learn to sing the music and words together. Then sing the music without the words, until it exists on its own. You have now been led by words to a vein of your own music. Sometimes the chariot of words will wheel you right past itself into the winged world of pure music. A poet friend of mine said, "Words take you so close to the truth because they are what led you away from it in the first place."

# There's Not Much to Learn and It Takes Forever

Music is made out of only a few simple atoms. There are two basic meters (duple and triple), two essential harmonic relationships (perfect fifths and major thirds), and two melodic motions (steps and leaps). There are a few expressive gestures (loud and soft), a few rhythms (dotted notes, syncopations), and a little scattered exotica. That's it. Why can't we learn it in a few weeks?

The truth is, a musician can spend a lifetime learning five notes and still not know everything in them. The more masterful you become, the deeper becomes the mystery and the more you are a beginner.

So when a student feels sluggish in learning a certain mode or cross rhythm, I have to say how there is hardly anything there to learn but that it takes more than one life.

Ingrained in our culture is the goal of sleek success. It is not a big surprise when students—especially adult students—are put off by how long it takes to learn simple things. "I become so aware of the part of me that thinks she ought to know how to do it," says a student. The reply: *there is no ought-to-know-how*, there is only the uncovering of ourselves when we sit at the polishing stone.

How can we shift our concentration away from fabulous others to the sweetness of inward discovery? Away from the goal and toward the ideal? Friend, you tell me.

# Dr. Overtone's Promise

If you want proof of the god of music, listen to the overtone series, the translucent aura of tones hovering above every musical tone. It is a proper object of devotion and a crucial tool for musical life. Although there are many books that describe it, and how to produce it, and how it organizes music, none of them goes far enough, in my opinion. None of them reads like the mystery thriller it is.

Sorry, but this book is not the overtone book. In compensation, I, Dr. Overtone, hereby promise the production of said book within our lifetimes. (Title: *The Book of Harmonic Experience.*)

Meanwhile, if you haven't heard them, have a musician who has show you the overtone series and don't give up until you hear overtones like trumpets. They are prophecy.

# Originality

There are two roads to originality: fast and high. The fast road is for the young and spry. It appeals to the side of us that wants to produce something entirely new, previously unimagined—a tinfoil dress, a recital from a hot-air balloon. This kind of originality, more properly called novelty, can be valuable. Indecipherable runes might lead us out of a maze. Bird talk can make listeners flap their wings, raising them up from their perches. When I was in my twenties a bunch of us Chicago boys found a way of improvising music from scratch, using theater game techniques. We made raucous, amazing music that went everywhere but up. It was fresh, aggressive, and fascinating. Now, twenty-five years later, I have left that music behind, but I am glad it happened because, its ephemeral beauties aside, it taught me what music is *not* in an extremely precise way. So the fast road can be a good one even if it leads to places you abandon later.

The high road is, of course, slow going. On its journey-man stretches we learn to love our traditions. We learn how to be apprentices and to love apprenticeship. We learn to imitate, or better yet, to steal every musical thing we love and use it for a while as if it were our own. We are struck by the similarities among humans. We are astonished to find the similarities greater than the differences. Eventually we are led to a quiet cave where we discover all of humanity inside ourselves. This turning inward to find the universal occurs at the steepest point of the high road, at the last hairpin curve opening up onto the ridge. The ridge, finally, is insight.

Like a zealot you follow the ridge where it leads you, no questions asked. It leads you to the truth about yourself.

Part of this truth is that you are everyone; the other part is that you are one-of-a-kind. The more you identify with humanity the more your uniqueness is revealed. In her lecture "The Question of Originality," Jane Hirshfield calls this uniqueness a "deep particularity."[4] It is deep like water flowing underground. *Origin* is from the Latin *oriri*, to rise, as in the rising up from earth of a subterranean spring. Originality rises from your underground truth. When you have passion for the truth about yourself, originality will percolate up through your work. When you go for the truth, originality takes care of itself.

In your passion to uncover yourself you become transparent; in that transparency your deep particularity becomes visible. "Originality," writes Hirshfield, "comes at its deepest level from a virtual transparency of the ego, in which the world and self open to each other. . . . Originality, one can say, is what you step out of the way of."

As the ridge leads you upward, your uniqueness comes into wider perspective. From the higher elevations you can see your whole life, and all the other roads and all the other lives on them, and how they are one road and one life. You can see how most of what you are has been given to you by the mere fact of your living, and by others who have lived before you. You realize that what is "original" essentially rearranges the familiar: the same ancient notes and gestures done over again in meaningful new ways. You realize that only the fingerprints are yours, and that this was true for Beethoven and his fingerprints, and Bird and his. You see how everybody is on the same pilgrimage, and how there is no racing on such a road as this. You desire one thing only: to be a conscientious traveler.

Do I advise one road over the other? I say, Take both roads at once! They are that kind of road. Part of you can be establishing a world speed record while the other part is resting beside a mountain lake gazing at the smooth stones on the sandy bottom.

# THE
# SOUND
# CONNECTION

# Finding a Teacher

When you are clear about what you want to learn, you will find your teacher. The teacher is already clear. The two of you will meet because you are looking for each other.

Old saying: When the student is ready, the teacher appears.

So your first work is to create a lucid picture of what you want. Here is an exercise.

Imagine yourself ten years into the future, making ideal music under perfect conditions. Allow no boundary to this vision, no editor, and no holding back. Try to capture the character of your future music in your ear, even if the notes are a blur. What is your feeling? What is the quality of the light? Notice who else is listening there with you. When the picture comes into focus, describe it in writing. Tell everything.

"I am in a woody kind of house with a dark brown decor. It is nighttime in the woods. I am sitting in a large living room full of nice furniture, in an easy chair, reading something, then composing something, then reading, then composing. The room has a high ceiling and there is a fireplace quietly burning. A soft receptive woman is in the room. I have a sweater on. My body has great vitality and my brain is clear and quiet.

"I am working in an interdisciplinary school where all the teachers are exploring the points where disciplines connect. I am a rhythm specialist with insights into psychology. I have studied acting. We are trying to bring about harmony to save the world. I have an understanding of music that leads to effective ways of working together. I am a light in the world."

The man who wrote that when he was twenty is now twenty-six and traveling with the San Francisco Mime Troop as a drummer and actor.

"I am in a sunny country house and I know how to play the piano in a way that makes me free. I am a healer. People come to me and I show them how they can play this way too, and they do, and they become whole, and this makes me really happy."

The forty-year-old woman who wrote that got her Ph.D. in psychology and is now, five years later, doing what she described.

"It is my fortieth birthday party. On an intimate stage in a little club I own, I am playing alto sax with a totally mellow jazz quartet. All my friends are there, listening intently. We play beautifully all night. Everyone has the best time of their lives and stays until dawn."

That was written by a new student, last week. We'll see.

Now try yours.

You can test your longing for the dream to come true. Go into the longing and ask: Why can't I do that now? Zero in on the inside reason. Feel your wanting. What has to happen for you to be that person you see?

Now: imagine the qualities of the person who can guide you there. That person is your teacher.

No such imagining preceded my meeting with the Sufi teacher Sam Lewis. Though I had observed him critically from a distance, I did not suppose my presence had registered with him. He was a radiant and loving being, but he could also be abrasive and boastful, and these are the qualities I chose to see. There was already plenty of that in myself; I did not need more of the same from this uncle type.

One day, at the consecration of a new spiritual center, all his followers are lined up at the lunch buffet to have their food blessed. Everyone is in high spirits, but I'm not buying anything spiritual. Of course, it certainly can't hurt to go through the line and have the old man bless my food. Besides, that appears to be the only way to get lunch.

Sam stretches both hands over each plate that passes in front of him, giving each student a deep and loving glance. OK, I can handle this. Now it is my turn. His hands are over my food; he says a prayer in a low voice. Then he snaps his neck all the way to the right, avoiding my eyes, and I hear a bright bell inside my skull. He is giving back to me the same energy I have been giving him. I feel the reflection inside of me. He has taken me on, resistances first, and at that moment I know he is my teacher.

When the right student shows up at my door there is sometimes a great inner joy. The violins swell upward and there are trumpets, even timpani, though all this is under the surface, as if part of a movie one remembers. The actual recognition scene is factual and mundane: "Yep, this is right."

But more often there is no fanfare. Like true love that grows out of plain friendship, the true student-teacher bond can grow out of casual (or even apparently negative) beginnings. Like a good marriage, it can be lifelong. Unlike marriage, it cannot be enriched by sexual intimacy. In a good marriage, both parties are student and teacher equally, or neither is either. In a formal student-teacher relationship, the student desires the role of apprentice and the teacher accepts the role of guide. There must be payment—either money or work—and clarity in that agreement.

Of course, all beings are your teachers: a tree is a teacher of treeness, a baby of babyness; and there are wind, rocks, adversity, and strangers. But I am referring to loving humans who lift us over the sharp stones or, with the same hands, push us headlong and caterwauling over the cliff.

Everyone has a book inside called *My Teachers*. I would like to mention those who have shaped my musical life so far: Buddy Hiles, the saxophonist (long dead); the composers William Russo and Easley Blackwood; Samuel Lewis; Hamza El-Din, the musician from Nubia; and the North Indian singer Pandit Pran Nath.

When you have found your true teacher, don't hide. Wherever he or she lives, go there, even if you have to take an airplane or hike into the wilderness; even if you go only occasionally. Whatever the fee, pay it, or work extra hours, harboring what you have until you can.

# Fear of Music

We can be afraid of anything: statues, love, moths, water. But I think we basically have two fears: death and our deep selves. Evan Eisenberg in *The Recording Angel*, commenting on the eeriness of listening to classical recordings, writes, "To face the dead is to face oneself; we do both when we face music. No wonder we fear true music, late at night, as much as we fear silence. . . . I am afraid to be alone with great music because I am afraid to be alone with my inner self. . . . I cannot find refuge from music in silence. Actually, fear of music and fear of silence are the same."[5]

Jane Hirshfield says that one of the Five Great Fears in Buddhist teaching is "fear of speaking before a large assembly. This fear of public exposure, of being found unacceptable if we speak honestly, if who we really are were to become known, is thus viewed as one of the major hindrances to enlightenment. . . . That the issue of self-revelation is given such prominence in religious teaching shows, in a way, that we should be compassionate to ourselves and understand how hard it really is to speak the truth."[6]

We are who we are. We die. There is no fear in writing those words or in reading them. The fear comes when we are a train rushing headlong into a tunnel with no possibility of escape. This can be exhilarating, but it is also frightening. Your true work as an artist inevitably places you on the track of your reality and your mortality. Ultimately, the track will lead through—and beyond—fear. The reason the obsessive

117

playing with paint, or picking at strings, or rearranging of words on a page leads beyond fear into sanity is that inside your personal reality is universal reality; when those colors and tones and words ring true for you they are, miraculously, true for others. If we penetrate the utterly personal we connect with everyone. At the end of your mortality is the continuity of life. At the end of your tunnel there is a light visible to all.

But try telling this to yourself when you can't concentrate on a particular passage of Mozart, can't get it right no matter what. Try convincing a painter there is visible light at the end of his tunnel when he is stuck twenty feet across the room from his canvas, or to a poet who is crumpling up the pages one by one.

Self-revelation is a hard business. The many forms of fear slow our bodies to a crawl and confuse our minds. We need a clue to recognize fear no matter the disguise. Our own resistance is that clue. Whenever you resist what you want to do, fear is present. Poor concentration is fear; procrastination, lack of coordination, diversionary tactics (hunger, doodling) are fear, fear, fear. Fear is not bad, mind you, it saves us from many a scrape. But unconscious fear is unconscious. Making the unconscious conscious is like opening your eyes in the dark, the work of waking up.

When you are at a stuck—really stuck—place in your music, there is a voice in that stuckness. It cries, "I don't have the talent to do this, I'm too old, I'm too dim, too slow, much too slow, plain unmusical, not worth the effort, whatever made me try this in the first place, who do I think I am, I'm worthless, I'm nuts, forget it." Listen to those cries. Home in on their location, so you can rush the velvet curtain, swatting it aside to reveal the drooling old actor backstage, at it again.

The most plaintive of these cries is, "I just don't have it." The way to crack that one is not through the *I* or the *don't* or the *have* but through the *it*. Put yourself on the hot seat.

Cross-examine yourself about the *it* you are expected to have. When was the *it* born? Who were *it's* parents? Is *it* a friend of yours? Are you sure? When did you last see *it* in person? Is *it* in the employ of another party? Can you name that party?

Artists must constantly guard against these hidden expectations that flap around their natural gift like dark birds. They must focus instead on polishing the jewels already in hand. In this lies salvation from a fearful life and, for musicians, the way to actual music. Enter the polishing! Love the refining of mere vibration, those waves on your very shore. You can latch onto a single musical sound as if it were a material ray flying you through frightened air. The ray will guide you. It is the *it* we all have, and it is enough.

# Hearing through Other Ears

The first time this happened to me I was a student of composer Easley Blackwood in Chicago; part of my apprenticeship was listening to him practice piano, often for many hours at a sitting. As our attunement grew, I found I could follow his practice routines and his patient polishing of passages under study. One fine day (actually it was three in the morning) I realized that I was on his wavelength. Not only was I hearing as he was, I was hearing through his ears.

This experience has recurred with my students as well as my teachers. Each time, it gives me the sensation of being rewired—as if I were at the receiving end of the other person's input signals. First there is the brightening that precedes a storm. Then, for a moment I seem to become the other person, heart and mind, while at the same time witnessing the scene. If that person is my teacher, the next step in my own path becomes illuminated. If that person is my student, the next step in my teaching of him or her becomes clear. The sense of connection is immediate and eternal. But it may also be one-way and entirely private. It is never necessary to discuss it with the other person.

I think this strange sensation is what happens when you listen long and quietly. It is a way of being helped, and of helping. It is an indication that music is sound coded for human purposes—a secret password that opens the borders between us.

Next time you are listening to someone play, let your own hearing fade back, and imagine for a moment that you are listening through the other musician's ears.

# Most Perfect Music

Ubud, Bali, 22 March 1989. As the sunset begins, I am writing on the balcony. Below me, flooded fields of new rice seem especially peaceful after the noisy weeks of harvesting and plowing. No herds of ducks, no tractors, no water buffalo, just curved sky and flat water. At the *banjar* (meetinghouse) about two hundred meters across the fields, a drummer is playing a hollowed-out log hung down from a crossbeam; its end has been slit so that it produces two pitches a small minor third apart. The drummer is sitting cross-legged on the floor, stroking the metabolism of an evening in love, sometimes waiting long seconds between strokes, sometimes setting a stately, even pace, almost always alternating the two pitches, whose hollow tones seem to stretch between and beyond the rice terraces. Roosters crow in the village beyond the *banjar*. Balinese language and a few English words rise from the long path; wind in the fronds and palms that line the riverbank. The glorious sky-blues and orange-pinks reflect up from the fields of lakes. Atmospheric harmony. Even the sounds are infused with quiet. With his carved stick, the drummer is beating in perfect rhythm, which means so in tune with the whole locale that you are never aware of him, yet the flux of his energy weaves the cloth. Within the quiet is another quiet. I can hear over the horizon into forever. I am more than myself, beyond my skin and my time.

The Slit Log Drum Piece lasted a half hour, until twilight. The guy was probably smoking and joking with his friends while he was playing, maybe absorbed in somebody's story, sipping some rice wine. The perfection of the music lay in the drummer's integration of everything around him, and the way he was audible to the whole village. He was hearing through his culture, through everyone's ears, as easily as we might tie shoes. The sound of his log drum was part of everything. And everything—people, trees, animals, water, sky—was part of the drum.

What I recognize, now that I am back in the thick of California, is how those two hollow tones functioned with the same completeness as, say, a Brahms symphony on a Sunday afternoon full of Boston concertgoers. Maybe the scene in Bali was already whole, so it needed only two tones to keep it together. Maybe our complex music needs all of its stitches to keep the cultural fabric from falling apart. Being on my own side of the ocean makes me want to hang on to that complexity, and identify with it.

But I did feel, at least once, entirely alive without it.

# The Circle of Listening

The sounds in your life are part of a circle of listening; a tiny arc on a great circumference. When you begin a note, it comes from somewhere and keeps going forever after you have finished. It comes from your impulse to sing, from your mind and heart, all the way back to the beginning of time. It goes into thin air, into walls, patient trees, open sky, molecules, heat, radiation, and on into vibrations there aren't names for. Part of it does, anyway. The rest of it goes into the hearts and minds of others. Nothing is lost. Everything keeps going around.

The soul knows all about circles. Its ears are bigger than elephant ears. Soul ears can track circles. They can tune in on the intention behind vibration, and follow *that* around.

Next time you hear music (maybe your own), tune in on the intention of the musician. What does this musician really want? To make you dance? To get paid? To sell money market certificates? To fill you with nostalgia? Longing? Light? Love? Mind? To praise God? To purge himself? To terrify you? To glorify violence? To show off? To get famous? To get laid? To assert territorial rights? The answer is audible to anyone listening.

Your intention is part of your music and never leaves it. It came from somewhere and goes somewhere. It is connected directly to your listeners and indirectly to everyone else. When the song is over, your intention keeps on going. Your inner work thus becomes inexorably mixed with the work of the world.

Your real work has inner light in it. When you know this light, public performance becomes luminous and joyous. Your music makes the little house where you live light up among the others. Your arc is a lighted life among lives. When your light shines back on you in a recognizable form ("I *loved* your concert") it has not gone far enough. Be patient. When it no longer has your name on it, you know that it has made its way safely into the nether regions of the Great Circle.

# Inner and Outer

Music practice lights up the inner life. The walls of your hidden rooms glow. In a new way you see how you are with yourself. When practicing, you notice how the everyday person feels in the presence of the secret person inside—comfortable, threatened, strange, or in love. The domestic who does the dishes clasps hands with the sage who guides from within. They gaze openly at one another.

The development of your musical language depends on the genuineness of this intimacy. There are times of peace and times of war. Peacetime is like a summer day in the country: the inner and outer worlds belong to each other. When the emotions of battle are storming through, however, you learn to handle them within the rules of the game, inside the art of it, inside the agreements drawn up between your selves. The level-eyed patient one watches over the wild one who grasps and flails; it's in the contract.

During all this, you are able to enjoy long visits with your own beauty. You are privy to your "deep particularity." You are uncovering the work that is yours and no one else's.

Music is not meditation or, ultimately, any other private act. Though it can be meditative and private—even selfish— eventually it, like any language, demands to be shared. For musicians, the safest place for sharing is the world of other musicians. We seek out one another, play for and with one another, have our own mores and our own slang. We are a mutual encouragement society. The impulse to play with friends grows like a vine stretching over a wall. It grows into the desire to play for everyone. Here is the juncture where you learn the most about your life—right here, in the turning outward from a private party of like-minded friends to the arena of public transmission.

What is needed for this outward giving is for the music to be authentically yours to give. Authenticity comes from the musical life, from the long hours spent polishing the lens of sound. A transparent lens has power in it. It becomes *your* power; you bring the light of music through. The stage fright of the pretender turns into the true lover's desire to give; that desire faces directly out into the big world.

Whether or not music is your primary work, a holistic view of your life does come into focus from music practice. The key is listening for your guidance, the inner part of you that knew this all along. When you connect with your guidance there are sparks from that recognition; you can feel them from the inside. From the outside, people can actually see the flashes of light in your music. Eventually, your inner friend comes to you openly *as* music. What begins as fireflies is finally a beacon. The sound of your music becomes a beacon leading to itself.

# Age Matters

There is no use crying over wasted time or limited gifts. I did. I spent my twenties learning formal music and being angry at my parents for not having found me a good formal teacher when I was five. The truth is I got what I got, which included, incidentally, a great jazz teacher when I was twelve.

Start with where you are, every time, no exceptions. Let your appreciation for what you already have become be preeminent. Then there will be an ecstasy to beginning something new, especially if you are old enough to see the arc of your life, and the circle it is part of.

You are never too old to learn music, or too young. The trick is to identify continuously with the act of self-discovery in the moment, not with the accomplishments of others, not with some *ought to* that has gotten stuck, like a seed in your teeth.

Age matters. You mature aurally. Your perception of sound opens and deepens. Your loves ripen, your hearing grows keener. You can read meaning where there was none before. You are wiser than you were even last week, and your heart and ears are bigger. Remind yourself to keep listening for the new in what seems to be the old and familiar. You may hear for the first time something that has been singing to you all along.

# Tone-Deaf Choir

Nobody is tone-deaf, but people who think they are (perhaps one in twenty) see themselves standing outside in the falling snow watching normal people in pretty houses singing at the dinner table. They think they are missing something everyone else has. When God was passing out ears, they were standing behind a door.

From time to time I teach tone-deaf classes. Such a class is best taught cooperatively by a man and a woman, in a group of about ten. So first I sign up a teaching partner. Then I advertise that I am looking for real turkeys, the ones who can't sing a note, couldn't carry a tune in a basket. The first day is spent sitting in a circle, each person telling his or her horror story:

"I'm the turkey you were looking for."

"No, that's *me*."

"I thought *I* was."

After a while it is clear that everyone has the same story to tell. There is a lot of laughing, whoops of recognition. Someone breaks down, everyone sobs. Relief—more laughing. By the time we have gone around the circle the collective story is rich with detail.

People learn at different rates of speed. If, in your early student life, you were slightly slower to perceive pitch relationship, it wasn't long before you were given, by your peers or an insensitive teacher, the identity of The One Who Can't Sing.

D'ya call that singing?

Stop that noise.

You be a hummer.

Why don't you sit here, where the others can't hear you?

Shut up.

Yuk on you.

Just move your lips.

My poor Sally couldn't carry a tune in a basket.

These cutting words came at the very moment Poor Sally was singing her five-year-old heart out. When we sing, the heart is alive in the larynx, and that narrow channel is highly sensitive to aggression. It takes only a small blow to cause big damage. Some unconscious little meanness, an offhand dig, might seem to a child like a slap on the heart, and the heart has a very long memory for pain.

This is deep pain. Singing is a special code that identifies us as human—our collective password. Not being able to utter the password is a kind of nightmare a child must live out during the daytime. Pretty soon we have a kid who can't sing and who feels partially ostracized. Then we have a grown-up, capable if not extraordinary in every way, who can't sing. Now there are ten of them sitting together, their woes going around the circle:

"When I sing I bring *everybody* down."

"I can really stop a party."

The worst thing the teacher can do is ask a person who thinks she is tone-deaf to match a pitch, especially a pitch struck on an instrument, especially the piano. For a man trying to match a woman's pitch it is additionally confusing because of the difference in register; likewise a woman trying to match a man's pitch. Even matching pitch man to man or woman to woman can seem threatening to someone with a tone-deaf identity. So the next step in our tone-deaf class is designed to rectify a mistake from the distant past.

First you point out the difference between a fluctuating tone and a nonfluctuating tone. A siren goes like this: (everyone make a sound like a siren). A dial tone goes like this: (everyone makes a sound like a dial tone). Now you ask a brave person to make, solo, a sound like a dial tone, but to take the nasal quality away, using instead the open vowel "ah." Is it nonfluctuating, that is, "even"? Everyone has the capacity to distinguish between a straight and a wavy line. Likewise, everyone can produce a nonfluctuating tone.

Now comes the magic part. If the volunteer is a male, the male teacher matches the volunteer's pitch. If she is female (or a child) the female teacher does the matching. Gently, receptively, the teacher breathes and sings with the student until both are singing a tone in precise unison. Something wonderful happens. Real tears come, all around. The human resonance of a true unison, the realization of connectedness, is what singing is all about, and the long-denied connection is now palpable. It is additionally powerful if the student puts her right hand on the teacher's breastbone; the teacher puts her right hand on the student's breastbone; and each covers the other's right hand with her own left hand. One by one you go around the circle, locked in breath, locked in vibration, locked in tune. An angel of mercy flutters above the class, which is at once hushed, amazed, boisterous, happy, nostalgic, cleansed, and full of memories. That is plenty for one two-hour class, or maybe two classes.

At a subsequent class, you might spend some time recognizing the anger inevitably harbored for the teachers, parents, and peers who knowingly or unknowingly did the damage. And a long, long moment forgiving them.

If gender-to-gender unison was magic, the next step is

trickery. The student now sings a "higher" tone followed by a "lower" tone. What the absolute pitches are does not matter, nor does their relation to each other. The important thing is that two comfortable, sustained tones are sung alternately. The teacher echoes the student. As soon as a predictable rhythm is established, the teacher surreptitiously takes two turns at once, so that the teacher is leading and the student is following. At this point the teacher says, "You're matching my pitches—I thought you said you were tone-deaf." Big laugh all around, and maybe some cheers. But the point has been made. If the teacher has taken enough cues from the student and has successfully emerged as the lead pitch, the student will match pitches. Not every time or flawlessly, but certainly. This is where much patience is needed. Bring people with you very slowly, from their need, not yours.

The next step is the riskiest, and it requires trust on all sides. You announce that everyone will now sing the same note. It might be best to split by gender, the woman teacher setting the pitch for the women (about middle C or B-flat), and the man teacher following with the men, an octave lower. Nine times out of ten everyone will be right there with no problem. If someone isn't getting it, guide that person's voice to the pitch, or even better, let that person set the pitch, which everyone else will then match. I've never had to stop long to herd strays; but if you do, you will find that the other students in the class have at least as much capacity for patience as the teacher, if not more. They will not be bored. The greatest sympathy is with the person who has the deepest pain, because it is everybody's pain.

A class of ten tone-deafers singing one pitch is a triumph, and the excitement is hard to contain. This is a marvel you can hear, and live inside of.

From this point on, music can be taught as if to beginners, though perhaps with more than usual consideration. Tune up a string or reed instrument to the chosen pitch, and open everyone's ears to the nature of the sound. Show the first two notes of a major scale. (I'll assume C major for now.) The teacher sings the simple phrase C–D–C and the class answers. Then many variations on two notes: C–C–D–D–C, D–C, D–C–D–C, and so on. Introduce B, so there are three pitches: one above the main pitch and one below. Now you have more musical possibilities. Try C–D–C–B–C and its many variations. Stay at this stage for a long, long time. Show the treachery of leaps: D to B is not as obvious as D to C. Use either the *do re mi fa sol la ti do* of European solfege, or the Sanskrit *sa re* (pronounced "ray") *ga ma pa dha ni sa* of Indian music. Some people have a kind of vertical dyslexia that confuses up and down. This goes away with deliberate effort. Work it out. That is plenty for another class or two.

At the next class, introduce E, so your scale now contains C, one note below it (B) and two notes above it (D and E). Now you can say, "Most music has only seven tones in it, and you can already sing over half of them."

Be sure to leave enough class time for people to report on the new feelings and experiences they have had during the week:

"I sang with the radio."

"My big sister said, 'I thought you were tone-deaf.' "

"My little boy wanted me to sing it again."

Over succeeding classes, teach stepwise melodies of two, three, four, or five notes. It is useful for a while to work with C–D–E–F as one group of notes, and (in the lower octave) G–A–B–C as another. The entire scale will emerge after many hours. From here, move on to songs, including nursery rhymes and pentatonic folk tunes ("Amazing Grace" is maybe the best), and improvised phrases. People will be astounded that they are creating their own melodies while naming the notes.

Toward the end of the cycle of eight or ten classes, simple part singing can be tried, the men holding one note while the women sing melodies, and vice versa. Choir fever sets in, catches hold, and rages. Cheeks flush. These are high times.

If people show sufficient interest they can, after the cycle has been completed, form a tone-deaf choir, become quite accomplished, and sing for hospitals and other service organizations, where the reception can be most warm and the circle of performance, singer to listener to singer, is joined.

Anyone who sings reliably on pitch, and knows they do, can help people who think they are tone-deaf, or even teach a class such as I have described. Long live the tone-deaf choir! May your banner fly forever!

# PRACTICES

# Singing in Unison with a String

In 1948, at a summer camp for boys on Lake Erie, the counselors entrusted with teaching us Rough Riders good dining room posture resorted, in cases like mine, to a board in the back. I was, at ten, a precocious hunchback. At table, my tongue hovered within striking distance of the peas on my plate. It wasn't long before I was required to eat a "square meal." A long, thin pine board, sanded and lacquered for this purpose, was inserted down my back under my shirt and tucked into the back of my shorts. Patriarchal cajoling combined with peer pressure caused my spine to flatten out against it. A properly grasped fork had to rise vertically from plate to mouth level, make a ninety-degree turn, and proceed horizontally (no spilling) into open jaws. On the return trip the empty fork retraced its path before mastication could commence.

This ceremony was accompanied by mock groaning and high hilarity, at least for the first few minutes. But after a while the boys piped down and the offender got through the meal with his back straight as a board, making the best of his humiliation. Of course, almost everyone had his turn eventually.

When I examine this memory it does not seem mean spirited. In fact, I have often wondered about the symbolism of board and spine. What is the meaning of the board? Is it an evolutionary absolute, a norm of perfection, or some jerk's idea? Why sit up straight, or carry books on our heads, or get all the answers right on the math quiz, or sing one tone precisely in tune with another? Why was the board grotesquely humorous? And was humiliation a necessary part of the deal?

As the boys of summer recede, we take charge of our own lives. We lay our spine against the board in a thousand different ways, one more creative than the next, more efficient, more joyous. And no, humiliation is not part of the deal.

A plucked string is the board, your voice is the spine. A lifetime of companionship can come from this straightening, this nurturing toward perfection.

When you study Indian music, your teacher shows you how to sing the first note of the scale, *sa*, against a string tuned to that note. When I first heard of this I thought, "How cosmic, how quaint." When I first started to practice it myself, all the resistances of an old lunchtime hunchback came flooding in. The boys would certainly groan and carry on if they could see me now. Old Board-in-the-Back at it again— careful lest your peas fall off your fork.

But all the boys were in fact busy with their own boards. I was alone with mine in my music studio looking at my watch and hoping I'd be perfect soon.

As in all disciplines, the act washes itself. Purity comes through doing. The voice trying to become level becomes the level voice. Emerging clearly from a forest of possibilities, this one practice has become the lacquered board of my life. It is a palpable guidance; it is animate. The string is the call. My unison with it, my willed resonance, is the answer. Singing in unison with a string is the musical practice of practices, the action from which the dramas and structures of music stream out.

If you want to do this practice you will need a stringed musical instrument, or some tunable source of sustained tone. Best among these is the tamboura, an instrument made in India for this purpose, but unless you live near a large coastal city or have contact with musicians from India (or their students), these are difficult to obtain. A guitar will work nicely, or any harplike instrument. Since you are seeking the relationship between your voice and a single string, it is best to dampen all the strings except the one you will use, either with your hand or with a strip of cloth. Striking a key on the piano is OK, though the hammer strikes of a piano are not as easy on the ear as the finger plucks of a guitar. Besides, every midrange note of a piano is actually produced by three strings at once, and unless the instrument is truly in tune, it is rare to find even one note where all three strings agree. It is best to locate a hands-on guitarlike string; piano is second choice. Instruments of the violin family work less well except in the case of trained musicians who can bow them expertly; the plucked sounds decay too rapidly.

Sounds from reeds are also a good possibility. An accordion, which is beautiful but unwieldy, or a concertina, could work. Indian musicians sometimes use a small box with a bellows and just a few reeds, called a shruti box. An electronic instrument like a keyboard synthesizer would be OK, with the right choice of sound: no vibrato, clean, kind to the ear.

Or you could construct a simple monochord type of instrument. Remember, all you need is a single string in singing voice range (or an octave lower). A beat-up old one-stringed abandoned guitar may at this moment be calling out your name.

Find a pitch you can sing comfortably, not too low. This generally falls around C, B, or A. Your drone must be tuned to that pitch, while still producing a full tone. You can sing sitting on a chair, or cross-legged on the floor, or standing, or in any comfortable position. Use the syllable *sa* with the vowel wide open. Find your breath and even it out. Relax your jaw, stretch your spine a little. Get hollow. Sound the drone and listen for a full minute. Listening is the key. Let the expansiveness of the drone's sound fill you up, even if it is soft. Take an ample breath and sing the drone's pitch within the sound of the drone, as though it were a round fruit and you were the sweetness inside.

The idea is to sing and listen at the same time, with equal energy. Receptive and expressive balanced; yin and yang on pirouette. To perfect that balance, to own it and identify with it, is the essence of music practice. Each *sa* is a chance to go up on point and make a controlled turn. On each breath, inside meets outside; sea meets shore. Find the rhythm of your breath and repeat the pitch with increasing awareness.

SOME PRACTICAL HINTS:

The notes should be not too long, not too short. Let your breath determine the length of the notes, one breath per note.

Try to begin each note at the *exact* pitch of the drone; don't scoop up to pitch like a motor revving up.

Give yourself a limit, and no further: two minutes? Eleven breaths? Twenty-one breaths? Maybe three today. Keep track on your fingers, not in your mind.

Ultimately, when lunch was over, everybody rewarded the board-in-the-back kid with a big cheer. This was an obligatory part of the ritual. It was as if the wheel of poor posture, board-straightening, and final approval had been set turning long before we were born, and we never questioned it.

But in music the work is its own reward; it cheers itself. It is good, after singing practice, to take a conscious moment to know that. These moments connect to one another.

# Just Any Note?

Practice is the art of constructing creative limits. A creative limit is like a box that seedlings grow in, or a pipe that increases the pressure of the water flowing through it.

I once taught improvisation at the San Francisco Conservatory of Music, in a course required of all incoming freshmen. The first exercise on the first day of class was called Ribbon. We would arrange ourselves in a circle with our various instruments. Each student would play a single note in turn, making a succession of single tones progressing around the room. After a while the exercise would transcend "it's my turn to play a note," and a ribbon of melody would emerge. Borne along with it would be the realization that music can be collectively improvised.

At the beginning of one such class, the circle halted at a sweet, shy violinist named Margit. She had undergone rigorous classical training in Sweden; this was her first week in San Francisco (in the early 1970s) and her first day of class. At the moment, she was standing with the bow frozen above her strings. "OK, Margit," I repeated, "when it's your turn, just play any note. We'll go around the circle again." Again, at her entrance, silence. Her freckled face had become crimson. When I asked if she understood my English she clenched her teeth and nodded vigorously. We tried again, but by this time her blush had become a pallor, and I thought she might faint. Still I was not patient. How could anyone, especially a trained musician, not understand such a simple rule? "Just play ANY

NOTE," I said. She filled her lungs with a gasp; her voice came from far away. "Just *any* note?"

A clear bell sounded in my head. I felt how the immensity of choice had flooded her with dismay. "No, not any note. Play any pizzicato note in second position on the D string." The breath she had been holding she exhaled with comprehension and relief. We went around the circle again; she played her note and eventually became a good improviser.

Each person needs different limits to set him or her free. Finding yours is what practice is all about. This is the most essential work of your teacher, though sooner or later you learn to invent useful limits for yourself. It is the most creative part of practicing your own music.

In the following chapters are various descriptions of such limits, beginning with those requiring less musical experience and then increasing in complexity. I hope they are musically fruitful, but I also want them to be examples of how limits are constructive.

# As Much as Possible
# from as Little as Possible

Practicing can be a game; the goal is a deeper knowing of musical sound. One strategy is to draw the greatest variety of music from the smallest amount of material: As Much As Possible From As Little As Possible—AMAPFALAP is the acronym. The prize is young blood for your musical characters, fresh color for your paintings. AMAPFALAP games are the kind master and beginner, both, can play with skill.

Here is a series of basic AMAPFALAP games.

## ONE NOTE

Pick a single note on your instrument or your voice, preferably midrange at first. Make a short piece using only that note.

Perhaps this one-note limit seems too austere, or maybe silly. But when you take it to heart you will find an astonishing array of possible sounds (without jumping octaves) including variations of:

dynamics (soft and loud)
duration (including silence)
timbre (color)
texture (how it would feel to your fingertips)

feeling and intention

There is a whole world in each of these dimensions. Let's look at them one at a time.

## Dynamics

To discover the *dynamics* of your note, play it as softly as possible, then as loudly as comfortable. Now play it repeatedly, starting from the soft end and working your way to the loud end while trying to distinguish each of these gradations:

very, very soft (*pianississimo*, abbreviated *ppp*)

very soft (*pianissimo*, pp)

soft (*piano*, *p*)

medium soft (*mezzo piano*, mp)

medium loud (*mezzo forte*, mf)

loud (*forte*, f)

very loud (*fortissimo*, ff)

very, very loud (*fortississimo*, fff).

This is not easy, though the best players can produce fifteen or twenty gradations. If you are a beginner, four or five is enough.

Usually, deeply felt music has a wide dynamic range. Rhythmic and melodic aspects of music are so compelling that it is easy to overlook dynamic shading. Less experienced players, in the heat of creativity, tend to settle at an unvarying loudness. Yet consider what a person communicates by speaking softly. Do we lean in to share a secret? Or is it some sort of subtle trick? Loudness might indicate righteous truth or a passionate lie. In music, the idea is to discover how loudness and softness can intensify the qualities of the notes. Beauty comes in when the qualities are mixed gradually, seamlessly, subtly, or suddenly.

## Duration

The *duration* of a note refers here not only to its length but also to the dark ground of silence that separates it from others. Repeated notes and the silences between them combine to produce a rhythm. The busy signal of a telephone is a simple example. There is also the nervous music of Morse code and the shrill work songs of computer printers. There is the living art of honking horns.

Rhythms can be random, but when a recognizable pattern does emerge it can become a building block in the musical architecture. Play your chosen note three or four times with some variety in the durations. Now repeat what you played; repeat it several times until it gels and you can remember it easily. You now have a block to build with. A lot of music can be generated from one rhythmic pattern, as the dot-dot-dot-dash of Beethoven's Fifth is often quoted to prove. Certain dances are associated with certain patterns, such as the samba. There are patterns so fecund that a whole culture identifies with them, like the bell rhythm of West Africa.

It is remarkable how these brief patterns can appear spontaneously. They are the common stuff of our environment, like gravel and grass. It is only when you sort them out, concentrate on them, and play them repeatedly that their magic emerges and glows. Find rhythmic patterns by experimentation and polish them with your own clear perception. Try mixing patterned passages with nonpatterned passages.

This universe of one note is growing fast.

## Timbre

The *timbre* of a note is the color of its tone, or the quality of its light when you listen with your eyes closed. Specifically, it refers to the recipe of overtones a note contains. Altering the recipe in speech produces the vowel differences in b*ee*t, b*ai*t, b*a*t, b*ough*t, B*u*rt, b*u*t, and boot. Altering the recipe on a string instrument can involve bowing (or plucking) at different points along the string; on a wind instrument, differences in lip pressure or air deflection; on a piano, use of the pedals. For some reason we are especially responsive to timbral variations when they occur in music—maybe precisely because they are so central to spoken language. You will find them on your instrument by seeking them out, and you will discover their aesthetics by falling like a baby into the sound of their sound.

## Texture

If timbre is something you can see, *texture* is the way music would feel to your tongue or the tips of your fingers if you could touch it. Sing a tone while buzzing "zzzz"; drape a chain necklace over the strings of your grand piano. Wind players know how to make their sound more or less airy, or to flutter their tongues. A rapidly alternating bow on a string makes the room tremble; greater bow pressure brings out the roughness of the resin on the bow.

A special kind of texture is the undulation called vibrato, a deep and rich resource. It is the difference between a hand running down your back and a hand running down your back caressing you with wavy little motions. Vibrato is a wave-like fluctuation in a tone's loudness (sing an even tone on the open vowel *ah* while covering and uncovering your mouth with your hand) or timbre (sing an even tone while pronouncing *yo-yo-yo* . . .) or pitch (let loose a high operatic tone and observe the natural rising and falling). These fluctuations can range from subtle to extreme, also from fast to slow. No other musical technique seems to bring us such warmth, or have such a human shape. The beauty is in the mixture of qualities. A jazz saxophonist's note, for instance, may begin without vibrato, but as the tone is held and the timbre darkens, a slow shallow wave is felt in the pitch, then another, faster and deeper; a third and fourth follow rapidly, but then the note brightens, levels out perfectly in tune, and disappears suddenly. Such techniques can scarcely be described—they are incandescent emotional responses of players. But you can become aware of vibrato by listening especially for it. You will find that opera singers and jazz singers are worlds apart in their use of it. So are classical violinists and jazz trumpet players, the women of Bulgaria and the men of Soviet Georgia (or American Georgia, for that matter, if they are singing shape-note hymns).

## Feeling and Intention

It is possible to observe directly, simply by concentrating, the effect of your *feeling*, or your *intention*, on the quality of your sound. Play a strident note; now one that caresses; now a sleepy one, for a lullaby. Search for your own qualities. Leaf through your emotional and psychic catalogue and see if a note saturated with feeling has a particular effect. It doesn't matter for now if you are imagining things or not. One of my old teachers used to say, "I don't care how you play it, just play it *some* way." If anger is close, check out angry notes. Or lovesick notes. Or an unnamed something. This is deep work.

At the end of this list of qualities let me add: *small pitch variations*. This is a great freedom. If you care to listen closely, and your instrument has variable pitch (most do; pianos don't), you can enter a volatile world by slightly raising or lowering the pitch at will. It is amazing how tiny pitch fluctuations can affect the energy of your whole body. By this subtle means, your single note might seem to appear from a dark register and disappear into a bright one; or to quiver in a one-note drama, a leaf snagged in an uneasy wind.

Now comes the best part: the cooking. All the ingredients have been tasted and tested. It is for you to make musical pieces that bring out the best results of their mixing. You can be the master chef and the gourmand at once, the mad chemist who can't explain anything, the alchemist who finds gold everywhere.

There are a few musical practices that can change your life; this is one of them. Never is the lesson of economy of means more efficiently or entertainingly revealed. The one-note AMAPFALAP is a special learning piece to be played over and over. It will never get old. You will never get enough. It is a house that is alive. It will never stop showing you what music is and what it does, and how you are in relation to it.


TWO NOTES: AFFLUENCE

When you first try this practice, choose a second note that is close to your original note (two or three half steps away) but not too close (one half step). For instance, assuming middle C has been your original note, choose the D right above it, or the E-flat; or choose the B-flat directly below it, or the A. Keeping alive all of the musical dimensions of the one-note pieces—dynamics, duration (or rhythm), timbre, texture, feeling—gradually work the second note into the mix. Maybe even try *avoiding* it until those moments when it will be most appreciated. Then reverse the roles of the notes so that the second is stressed and the first is scarce. Now let the second function as a grace note ornament to the first. Now reverse these roles. See if you can make a short piece that naturally comes to rest on the lower note; now likewise adjust the relationship so that the piece comes to rest on the upper note. Can you create a balanced relationship such that the piece might end just as convincingly on either note? Mostly, just play—make music. The two notes may become like two characters in an opera, or two sides of your own nature. They can take on personality and remind you of the way two people can exchange roles, can yin-and-yang each other. (This is especially true if you sing the piece.) Or, they may become an endlessly fascinating puzzle of proportion and symmetry.

On some instruments the notes can be articulated simultaneously, perhaps with different qualities (one loud, one soft; one staccato, one sustained). Would a trill make a good climax? or ending? Don't forget what a friend silence is to music.

There is a character unique to each pair of notes. Try two notes a perfect fifth apart (C and the G above) or a minor seventh apart (C and the B-flat above). As you practice these various combinations, their big magic and little magic will spin out. I heard some enormous minor-third magic once, which is described in the chapter "Most Perfect Music."

THREE NOTES

Again choose notes fairly close together, at least to begin with. Some combinations have appeared more frequently than others in the world's music. Here are some universally used sets (using C as the reference note):

C D E
C D F
C Db E
C Db F
C Eb F
C E F

There are many other possibilities, and they are yours to discover. Any of the notes can be made to sound like the central note of its set.

With three notes you will begin to discover the melodic conventions that typify music wherever it springs up, the rise and fall we love to ride. Tune and themes appear and reappear, shaping the music. For instance, suppose your set of notes is C–E-flat–F; and that you have played C–E-flat–C–F–F–F, fairly loudly. Now play the same phrase fairly softly; and then once again very, very softly, as if from a great distance. Improvise a piece featuring several recurrences of this thrice-played theme.

There is also the possibility of two- and three-note chords, used as punctuation or as a texture for themselves. *But*—the more intrigued you become with the increasing number of pitch possibilities the easier it is to forget the subtle shadings of texture and feeling that were essential in the good old days when there was only one note. Don't lose that world! Now is the time to play another one-note piece, as a reminder.

## FOUR NOTES

Much of the world's greatest music is made with only five notes, and here we are already playing with four. Four notes may not seem like a lot, but when you are inside them they can make a profound and sophisticated pitch language. Here are a few of the most likely sets, out of dozens of choices. This time, begin and end on C, and let your melodies revolve around C.

B♭ C E♭ F

B C D E

A C D E

G C D E

C D E G

C E♭ F G

C D F♯ G

C E F G

C E♭ G A♭

C F G B♭

The chordal possibilities are great: two, three, or four notes at once in many combinations with many textures.

It is easy to assume that music of limited means (four tones as opposed to seven or twelve; one flute as opposed to a symphony orchestra) is necessarily limited in complexity or quality. Not so. Indeed, some of the music that employs a huge vocabulary of sounds is not only inane but ironically so, since the contrast between a luxury of means and impoverished results does not escape notice. One thing that AMAP-FALAP games can do for you is sensitize you to ancient musics (like African or Chinese) that have not lost that magnificent delight in achieving more from less.

## All the Octaves

As an extension of four-note music, observe the effect of the four notes when you use all of the octaves available on your instrument. If the notes are B, C, D, E, for instance, then you could use any B and any C and any D and any E in any combination in any octave. This gives the possibility of wide melodic leaps and, on keyboards, widely spaced chords, including atmospheric or thunderous effects. For example: strike those four notes as a cluster around middle C softly and simultaneously. This has a different feeling than when you play the B an octave higher and the E an octave lower, making the following chord: E (below middle C), middle C, the D directly above it, and the B above that. Perhaps more basically, the melodic phrase B, C when the notes are adjacent means something quite different from when the C is struck an octave higher. You can practice playing simple melodies in a compact range and then displacing by an octave just the right note at just the right time, to give a sudden sense of flying, or enlarged space.

# Touch What You Sing

At the heart of melody is inner hearing. Here is a practice that connects inner hearing with the physical exertions of music making. It is for players of all melodic instruments, but it is most easily described as a keyboard exercise. It is for musicians of every level of development, even advanced players who think they already know how to do it.

The exercise is in a particular key and mode (for now). Let's choose the key of C and the major mode: on the piano, the white notes beginning on C.

1. With your right hand strike middle C. Then strike D. Play a brief melody comprised of these two notes only. For instance, C D D C D D C C.

2. Continue improvising using these two notes only, but now sing what you are playing. Women sing in the octave you are playing; men an octave lower. Get used to singing the pitches at the same time you play them. As much as possible, blend your voice with the sound of the instrument.

3. Expand to three pitches: C, D, and E. Believe you are simultaneously singing and playing short passages of real music.

4. Continue as before, but instead of pressing the keys all the way down, merely touch them. The only sound is the sound of your singing, even though you are going through the motions of playing the instrument. You are touching the keys and singing the notes that would sound if you were striking the keys. If you become unsure of the accuracy of the note you are singing, strike the key as a check. Don't sing D and touch E. Sing what you touch.

5. Here is the payoff: allow the singing impulse to predominate. *Touch what you sing.* Let your instrument become an extension of your singing body. If there is a disagreement between what you are touching and what you are singing, follow your voice every time. This is the high road to music. It gives priority to the inner world and asks the outer world to mirror it faithfully.

It is surprising that even with this small set of notes you may be unsure. Get sure. This is a crucial turning point in music making, the step most usually omitted in our culture's teaching. Practice with three notes until you can sing them with certainty, touching what you sing. The mastery of this is never great enough. The work is to become more and more graceful in this most basic of musical gestures.

6. Add B below C. If you make too many mistakes, play and sing only stepwise, that is, only notes that are next to each other. Avoid leaps (B up to E, or D down to B, for example) until all the stepwise motion (like B to C, and D to C) is smooth. Don't be in a hurry; this is a life of work.

7. As you continue, with your left hand quietly sound the C below middle C and keep that sound in the air by occasionally restriking that key. This will stabilize what you are singing and encourage you to sing in tune.

8. Gradually add more white notes as you can. Eventually you will be singing all the notes of a C major scale throughout the compass of your vocal range, touching what you sing.

If you are a reed player, instead of touching the keys of a keyboard operate the keys of your instrument without sounding the reed. If you are a brass player, play the valves. If you are a string player, use the fretboard or fingerboard only.

Of all instrumentalists it is the pianist whose connection with melodic line is most in jeopardy. From the beginning we are confronted with a sleek machine. We never touch the strings. We stimulate our intellects with counterpoint and harmony and scarcely hear the longing of the wood in our instruments to return home to the forest. We of all musicians have to use our own voices to remember the melodic longing.

This exercise ranges from very easy (two notes with simple rhythm) to extremely difficult (several octaves, with rapid, leaping figuration). As long as you are honest with your knowing and your not knowing, the world of melody will unfold regardless of your level of musical development. You can expand the procedure by using a mode other than major (stay in the key of C, but use B-flat instead of B, or F-sharp instead of F, or E-flat instead of E) or a key other than C, but you do not have to do either of these to receive the benefits.

The benefits appear slowly, over many years. You know you have the full blessing when your free inner voice is the core of every note. No deep musician could ever play what is not being sung inside. Music begins there. Then the player touches her instrument, and the inner world leaps out for a flickering life in the outer one.

# *Steps/Leaps*

Understanding melody begins with the distinction between steps and leaps. Our scales have seven tones—no one knows why. They are named in alphabetical order according to a seven-letter alphabet. You *step* from a scale tone to an adjacent scale tone. You *leap* over a scale tone, or over several.

Here is a stepwise melody: C D E D E F E F G A G F E D E D C.

Here is a melody of mostly leaps: C up to F down to D up to G down to C up to A down to F up to B down to G up to A down to C.

Sing both. An axiom emerges: Steps are easy; leaps are hard.

This means that stepwise melody sounds logical and naturally contoured, as if one could easily draw a line through the dots made by the notes. A leap, on the other hand, is a special event, which the ear singles out. A leap is a dramatic moment, a roughness to be made smooth by the surrounding stepwise motions. A melody full of leaps will be angular, difficult to sing and to hear, fighting with itself for the spotlight—though not necessarily the less beautiful.

*Corollary*: Some leaps are harder than others. It is not especially difficult to hear an octave (C to the C above it) or a fifth (C to the G above it). Sixths and sevenths are almost always more difficult.

*Second corollary*: Leaps tend to get filled in. If you leap from C up to F the chances are great that the intervening E and D will soon appear. "Somewhere over the Rainbow" beings with the upward leap of an octave and spends the rest of the refrain artfully filling in that octave while making other, smaller leaps and filling *them* in as well.

My advice: Learn to improvise predominantly stepwise melodies at first, passing time and gaining confidence in the stepwise flow. Bring in leaps gradually, as dramatic events, and notice how you backfill what you leaped over. Appreciate how this simple distinction enables you to get around, to recognize the ridges and valleys of your own melodic country.

# The Tyranny of Triads

Triads are every-other-note chords, like C–E–G (C major) and C–E-flat–G (C minor). For generations we have been taught that the twelve major triads and the twelve minor triads are the building blocks of music. All the names for all the note combinations reflect this every-other-note principle. If something is a triad, or resembles one, it exists and it has a name. If it does not resemble a triad, it doesn't have a name and it might not be thought to exist. These days more musicians are thinking that the basic building blocks of music are the degrees of the scale and their relation to the first degree of the scale. Of course, these degrees do combine into chords, and triads are the most consonant kind of chord. But not the only kind.

Be sure not to confine your chord search to the conventional major and minor triads. There are many beautiful and useful nontriadic (and quasi-triadic) combinations. Here are some based on C (spelling upward):

C D G
C F B♭
C G D
C D B
C A B♭
C A♭ B
C D♭ B♭

These can be transposed to any pitch, of course.

Don't be too comfortable with conventional wisdom. Feel free to search for unusual combinations. A chord that seems sour at first may prove intoxicating, like wine.

# The Art of Returning

One of the most enjoyable forms for the improviser is the *rondo*, a piece of music made up of several sections, described symbolically as *A B A C A D A E*, and so on. The A is called the *return*. It is interspersed with new material—*B, C,* and so on—called *episodes*, which are different from each other and from the return. The first task is to make up a recognizable phrase to which the music can convincingly return.

Although in the classical tradition the return is a group of related phrases, in improvisation it need be only substantial enough to catch the ear—perhaps just a few notes played in some distinctive way. Making up such a phrase is not as difficult as remembering it.

Here is a chance to memorize a phrase of your own music so well that it will reappear instantly when called upon. You may write the phrase down of course, if you know how, or tape it. But neither is necessary. In any case, you may be surprised at how elusive a phrase of music can be. Music was invented slippery.

The episodes that alternate with the return must contrast sufficiently with it. They can even give an impression of coming from another piece entirely. An astonishing axiom of music is this: It doesn't matter where you go, it only matters how you get back. So, after stating the A section once, take some wild leap. Change key, change texture, change feeling. Then gradually and patiently guide that music back, transforming it by stages into the music of the return. It is in this

161

guiding-back process that the rondo form will teach you most generously.

After a certain number of episodes and returns, the piece will seem finished. Perhaps you will need an extra flourish, or a final sigh.

There is a sweet kind of energy that runs between fresh, new music and music made familiar by repetition. When you put together a rondo this energy becomes part of you.

# Juice between Textures

Here is another good form for improvising short pieces.

Play something. Call that Texture One. Then reach for a completely different sound, well contrasted with the first. That is Texture Two. The piece you will play consists of the mutual influence of these two textures on each other, their dialogue, their gravitational bending. Maybe one wins out over the other. Maybe they become absorbed in each other. Maybe their intermingling generates a new idea. Energy from two opposed or highly contrasted ideas creates a flow of musical juice, like current between electrodes.

Remember the parameters of contrast: loud-soft, high-low, fast-slow, consonant-dissonant, dense-sparse. A low, slow, sparse passage (for instance) contrasting with a high, fast, dense passage opens up a middle ground where musical events can take place. Of course, more subtlety in the contrasts will yield more subtlety in the unfolding of the play, up to a point. Your work is to discover the ideal relationship between two textures. When you find it, your piece will tell its own story and play itself out to the end.

# Play by the Clock

Music fills up time like paint fills up canvas. So much canvas, so much paint. So many seconds, so many notes. Just as it is OK to say, "Now I am going to paint a picture that is eighteen by twenty-four inches," it is also OK to say, "Now I am going to make a piece that lasts one minute." It is a freeing exercise, one that teaches you about proportion.

Sit down with a clock or watch (a digital chronometer is best) in front of you. Play a piece that lasts one minute.
At thirty seconds, realize "one-half done."
At about forty seconds, realize "if it is going to happen it had better be soon."
At fifty-five seconds, "land this sucker."
Try to come in at exactly sixty seconds.

Now improvise a totally different one-minute piece.
Now another.

The time constraint opens something up wide. The secrets of composition come rushing at you. You begin to realize the consequences of your actions. One long minute becomes a life, and when that one is over there is another life. Music has this power—one complete life after another.

# Just the News

Here is an improvisation that's good to play for a friend.

Remember a little scene you were in within the last forty-eight hours, or that you witnessed:

A bag lady gets on the bus, can't come up with the money; the driver kicks her off at the next stop.

Your best friend leaves for the Middle East.

You dream about your first love.

The nasty mailman is nice for once—today is his birthday.

The event may not seem in any way extraordinary. As long as it has moved you, as long as the current of feeling is still flowing, it will serve as the raw material for this piece. Whatever comes to mind first is probably best.

Sit your friend down. Close your eyes. Take a few seconds to relive—*really* relive—what happened. Do not verbalize it.

Improvise a short piece that is like a journal of the event, telling the story truthfully on your instrument.

End of "Just the News."

You still don't have to say in words what happened, unless you want to.

# The Magic Scale

As a culture we love seven-tone scales (the eighth tone being the octave) as in *do re mi fa sol la ti do*. There are various theories of why our ears choose seven as opposed to six, eight, or nine, but in the end it is just something that is true: our ladders have seven rungs. Although on conventional instruments there are twelve tones to the octave, typically we use only seven of them at a time. Considered all together, the twelve are called a *chromatic scale*. A *mode* is a specific set of seven chosen from the twelve. The name of the tone that the set begins on and gravitates around identifies the *key*.

There is a system for choosing the seven tones. Knowing the system makes available a universe of conscious possibilities.

Again, we begin with the note C and use the major mode (the white keys on the piano) as a reference. The seven tones of the C major mode give us these unambiguous letter names to work with: C D E F G A B (plus the octave C). The question can now be asked: How can the remaining five tones (in this case, the black keys) be used?

The answer: C will always be considered the first rung, or *degree* (to use the musical term). And G will always be considered the fifth degree. Hence, the first and the fifth degrees are fixed for all the modes included in this discussion.

For the second, third, fourth, sixth, and seventh degrees of our C scale, however, we have a choice between pairs of notes, as follows:

For the second degree, there is a choice between D♭ and D.

For the third degree, between E♭ and E.

For the fourth degree, between F and F♯.

For the sixth degree, between A♭ and A.

For the seventh degree, between B♭ and B.

Here is another way of writing it:

C   D♭/D   E♭/E   F/F♯   G   A♭/A   B♭/B   C

Thus organized, these notes have extremely special—one might say magical—properties. I'll demonstrate how to use them by constructing a mode that reflects my mood at this moment.

First degree: C is given.

Second degree: my choice is D.

Third degree: I choose E♭ (seems to go with the overcast sky).

Fourth degree: I choose F♯ (the light is welcome).

Fifth degree: G is given.

Sixth degree: My choice is A.

Seventh degree: I choose B♭ (complements the E♭, according to my mood).

Eighth degree: C again, an octave above the starting note.

My mode, and mood, of the moment is C D E-flat F-sharp G A B-flat C. As far as I know there is no name for this mode, but the bottom half looks like a mode called gypsy minor, and the top half looks like one called dorian, so I'll call it gypsy-dorian. I guess that's the mood I'm in. To make music from it, I will proceed as in "Touch What You Sing," resting from time to time on either of the fixed tones, C and G, working my way through the modal terrain, investigating melodic pathways through many octaves that lead somewhere or nowhere, and being conscious of the relationships characteristic of this particular set of tones.

If I am a keyboard player I will try to keep C and G sounding quietly in the bass. If I am a guitarist I will either play in C open tuning or transpose the entire scale to D and play in D open tuning.

*Mode* and *mood* have a related etymology, which means that the mode you play conditions and is conditioned by the way you feel. Mode is a direct translation into sound of mood, of indescribable feeling.

Now construct a mode of your own choosing, and improvise inside of it. There are 32 seven-tone modes available from the material of the Magic Scale. About half of them work like crazy, about a third of them are difficult but very workable, and a few are problematical, but not unmusical. Take your chances, and if you feel stuck, change something.

Six of the possible modes are conventionally taught as basic music theory. They are generally more accessible in that they sound more or less familiar to us. They are listed below, along with their apocryphal Greek names, ranging incrementally down the page from a sunny quality to a moony quality.

| | | | | | | | | |
|---|---|---|---|---|---|---|---|---|
| C | D | E | F♯ | G | A | B | C | (Lydian) |
| C | D | E | F | G | A | B | C | (Ionian, the same as our major) |
| C | D | E | F | G | A | B♭ | C | (Mixolydian) |
| C | D | E♭ | F | G | A | B♭ | C | (Dorian) |
| C | D | E♭ | F | G | A♭ | B♭ | C | (Aeolian, our natural minor) |
| C | D♭ | E♭ | F | G | A♭ | B♭ | C | (Phrygian) |

It is an illuminating exercise to play for a few minutes in each of these modes, progressing in order from Lydian all the way down to Phrygian, and then working back up to Lydian again, and feel the mood, and quality of light, change. I said sunny to moony, but don't take my word for it.

All of these modes have been discussed as starting from C, for convenience in naming the pitches. But of course any mode can start on any pitch, and musicians spend many lifetimes learning to perceive the entire modal panoply from each note on their instrument.

Learning each of these modes is in fact a profound work. No one learns them overnight, or in a year. Each has a secret shape that needs to be worked like adobe into a house of your own making. Go slow, slow. Great musicians sometimes choose only a few modes and stay with them over a lifetime of dedication. Each mode is as recognizable as the face of a friend and, as with a friend, a deep feeling of kinship can be cultivated. Each has a full heart and a soul to reveal. Be cautious and respectful. These tones are alive, and they return your love.

# BIG EARS

# Big Ears

In earlier years, when I first began to go to the concerts of my teacher Pandit Pran Nath (he's still singing), I noticed flowers everywhere, incense, and clean white clothes. A thin brown man sitting cross-legged on a rug would sing North Indian classical music for two hours in front of forty or fifty devoted listeners. The air filled with honey. Our borders melted. We merged into flickering light. Our ears got big.

After the concert, people would stand around, quietly smiling. "Thank you, Guru-ji."

"Thank you."

"Thank you so much."

He would reply, in Hindi-accented English, "Everything is God," or in Arabic, "Ya Malik," God is King.

In those same years, I often gave day-long seminars followed by a concert at night. The seminars were to help people find the next step in their music making. At the end of the day people would stand around and say, "Thank you, Allaudin, I'm so glad I came."

"Thank you so much."

"Thank you, thank you, this was really helpful."

In the evening, after a concert of my own improvisations, people would stand around and say, "Very interesting."

"Interesting."

"You play very interesting music, young man."

"Very interesting, Allaudin."

This went on for years. Something was wrong.

About a dozen years ago I gave such an all-day seminar, followed by an evening concert, in Boston. There were about twenty-five people at the seminar. Afterward they stood around and said, "Thank you, Allaudin."

"I got something I really needed. Thank you."

"Many, many thanks."

My evening concert was in the recital hall of the Harvard University Music Department. I had been practicing well and was in fine form. As it happened, there was a huge blizzard that night, and only fourteen people showed up. But I was inspired by the gorgeous Steinway and the intimacy of the small crowd. At the end of the concert, people stood around and said, "Very interesting, Allaudin."

"Interesting music."

"I was very interested."

I was staying that evening with a friend of mine, a Sufi teacher. We drove home calmly through bright streaks of snow lit by the headlights. He waited until the heater warmed the car, then asked me what I thought about the concert.

"I liked it. I played well. But people don't seem to share my high opinion. You know, it's a funny thing." I frowned in the dark. "After Pandit Pran Nath's concerts, people say, 'Thank you, thank you.' After my seminars people say, 'Thank you, thank you.' After my concerts, people say, 'Very interesting.' "

I realized I was angry. "Guru-ji sings: 'Thank you.' I teach: 'Thank you.' I play: 'Very interesting.' Teach: 'Thank you.' Play: 'Interesting, very interesting.' If one more person tells me my music is interesting, I'm going to kill myself!"

I saw the lighted crystals falling into the windshield as if I had just woken from a coma. They slanted in from the void, from dark impersonal nature. I might as well have been on

Neptune. The universe could get along quite well without me. I was stunned by what I had said.

We drove slowly for a while over the white blanket, the car remarkably quiet. My friend said softly, "What is the purpose of your life?"

I must have been ready to hear the question, because my entire life did become coherent in that moment. I saw that my mission had been to compress the world's music into a personal style, to squeeze the wisdom and beauty of cultures into a many-colored ball, which I threw into the air to win esteem from my listeners. I had thought of myself as a clearing house for the world's brains, a switching center for cultures, a touchstone. I had studied everything and could demonstrate interrelatedness on all levels. I could use African and Asian and European essences the way Beethoven used themes, and weave a planetary counterpoint, *spontaneously*, to show that it could be done and that I could do it.

Naturally, people found that very interesting.

My teaching had taken quite another tack. Teaching had been kind to me, a good income, a gentle way of supporting my art. I never developed it methodically, just did the best I could to help people whatever the circumstances. To help people, whatever . . .

Ah.

*What is the purpose of your life?*

In teaching, the act of showing off or parading my abilities would be obscene. The object of teaching is to bring others forward, to set useful examples, to foster self-confidence and a love of the medium. You learn to listen to students—not with musically big ears, which recognize pitches and key changes, but with the Big Ears of compassion, which recognize desire and pain.

Of course people said thank you.

Now, rolling through Boston, I realized that my music

had gotten stuck because I was trying to prove something. Too much ego in it. I hadn't stepped out of the way. Whereas in teaching I did get out of the way—I had nothing to prove. I just gave. Now I had to learn to give my music away. My friend's question framed teaching and music-making into one and the same life, a helping life.

I began to hear music differently. I began to hear something in bare sound I had never heard before, to experience in the very act of hearing an upward intention, as if some current were drawing us toward it. I learned that sound is alive. I learned that sound *itself* is a purposeful life, and that music is the evolution of that purpose. I found my own purpose hidden in the swell, my pure chord in the roar of waters. My music and my life began to grow reciprocally, like longtime lovers who grow to look alike.

Life purpose evolves through a hundred million strokes, through the necklace of stroked and plucked and blown notes that stretches around the moon and back again. Stroke by stroke, your ears are tuned to the heart of the world, and when you are ready, you give away all of the strokes, everything you have learned. Your ears grow huge and, finally, you give them away too. The tables are turned. Music is hearing you. Music plays you.

A miller grinds wheat all day. By sunset he has a bag of perfect white flour.
The flour says, "Are you fine enough yet?"
He takes the flour to be baked into bread.
Next morning the bread comes steaming hot out of the oven and says to the baker, "You certainly look delicious to me."

The secret of big ears is remembering—remembering to listen. When we forget, circles break into fragments, inner and outer keep to themselves.

I do not know why we are so forgetful.

Teachers have been telling me to observe my breath for twenty years, but I cannot remember to do it for more than a few minutes at a stretch. "Remember to listen" sounds easy, but try to do it for half an hour while living life. These sayings fade in and out.

I guess we have a lot to do. No single thing fixes everything. But don't you feel full and round when the fresh bread loves your mouth? There is no end to where that love goes.

# Notes

1. *Science News*, vol. 138, no. 13. p. 196.
2. Anita T. Sullivan, *The Seventh Dragon* (Portland, Ore.: Metamorphous Press, 1985). p. 95.
3. Translations of the work of Jelaluddin Rumi courtesy of Coleman Barks.
4. Jane Hirschfield, "The Question of Originality," in *The American Poetry Review*, vol. 18, no. 4. Used with permission.
5. Evan Eisenberg, *The Recording Angel* (Penguin: 1988). pp. 60, 203.
6. Hirschfield, "The Question of Originality."

# RECORDINGS BY W. A. MATHIEU

Solo Piano Albums
   *Streaming Wisdom* (1981)
   *In the Wind* (1983)
   *Second Nature* (1985)
   *Listening to Evening* (1986)
   *Available Light* (1987)
   *Celebration* (1990)

Musical Settings of the Poems of Jelaluddin Rumi
   *In the Arc of Your Mallet/Quatrains* (1988)
      Text translated by Coleman Barks. Composed by W. A.
      Mathieu. Sung by Devi Mathieu and members of the Sufi
      Choir, with W. A. Mathieu, piano.

Available from:
   Cold Mountain Music
   P.O. Box 912
   Sebastopol, CA 95473

*The Listening Book* is available as an audio tape from:
   Shambhala Lion Editions
   P.O. Box 308
   Boston, MA 02117-0308
   (617) 424-0030